Wittgenstein
on Words as
Instruments
Lessons in Philosophical Psychology

J. F. M. HUNTER

Wittgenstein on Words as Instruments

Lessons in Philosophical Psychology

EDINBURGH UNIVERSITY PRESS

© J. F. M. Hunter 1990
Edinburgh University Press
22 George Square, Edinburgh

Set in Linotronic Melior
·by Koinonia Ltd, Bury, and
printed in Great Britain by
Redwood Press Limited
Melksham, Wilts

British Library Cataloguing
  in Publication Data
Hunter, J. F. M. (John Fletcher
  MacGregor), *1924*–
Wittgenstein on words as
  instruments : lessons in
  philosophical 'psychology'.
1. Psychology. Theories of
  Wittgenstein, Ludwig, 1889-
  1951
I. Title
150.92

ISBN 0 7486 0163 5
ISBN 0 7486 0194 5 pbk

CONTENTS

Part 2

Part 3

PREFACE

Although this monograph is ostensibly about a fairly well-known theme of Wittgenstein's, any reader of part 1 will surely be struck by how infrequently Wittgenstein is mentioned, and how much the discussions have the style and character of someone presenting his own deliberations about any of the topics discussed – rather than the character of an exercise in sleuthing out the views of an author whose prose is not easily understood.

Whereas it would seem fair to expect that I would be primarily at work on questions such as 'How did Wittgenstein handle the subject of believing?' 'What did he mean when he said we can't mistrust our belief?' and so on, on the contrary most often I first off present my own way of dealing with a question, and only then turn to consider how far Wittgenstein might have agreed. In this way my approach to questions of interpretation is in a sense indirect: faced with a hard question such as why Wittgenstein says that pain is neither a something nor a nothing, I do not so much look for clues in the surrounding text, or in other of his writings, as construct a theory of my own about how some puzzlement about pain might be cleared up by recognizing that in an imaginable sense of 'a something', our difficulty about pain has arisen from supposing that it is a something, and that this is a mistake.

It would not be all wrong to liken this aspect of the way I go about this kind of work to Plato's strategy for deciphering small handwriting: produce a clear formulation of what the burden of the script *might* be, and then consider whether *this* mark can be seen as the 'h' it would have to be, to verify the hypothesis that the script was saying such and such, and whether *this* could be the 'a', and so on.

Although I am, in ways like this, trying to work out a clear and justified account of what Wittgenstein was up to in this place and in that, I am less interested in that project than in working out ways of getting to the other side of philosophical difficulties. I say 'getting to the other side' because that expression seems to me to cover both the attempt to solve problems, and the attempt to dissolve them, to show it was a mistake to have been puzzled. Wittgenstein reckoned he knew a good deal about dissolving problems, and indeed may have thought that this is all that can be done in his kind of philosophy; but I want to leave room for the possibility of *solving* some problems, even if I cannot suggest problems that are clearly philosophical and have been or might be solved, and even if such philosophical skills as I have run almost entirely in the direction of dissolving difficulties.

As will be abundantly clear from Part 1, I am always more than willing to gratify Wittgenstein's wish that his writing should not save other people the trouble of thinking for themselves. It may be that, setting out on my own the way I so often do, I go too far, either in making points that some people may feel would never have been made by Wittgenstein, or in discussing notions (pleasure and deciding, for example) about which, to my knowledge, he had nothing to say; but I make no apology for this. I think it is important to show to what a rich array of concepts, many of them scarcely discussed elsewhere in philosophy, the Witgensteinian techniques and devices I am describing and using apply; and I particularly want to show how many different kinds of tactic may be needed, to divest us of our perplexity in various cases. Words turn out to differ more from one to the next than we might have expected, and hard work and craftsmanship are needed, to do a proper job.

When Wittgenstein said (*Philosophical Investigations* §133)
> there is not *a* philosophical method, though there are
> indeed methods, like different therapies

I take him to have meant, not that his philosophical methods either are therapies, or are like them in some ways, but only that, just as there are different therapies and one will want to treat cancer differently from schizophrenia and tennis elbow, so likewise there are different philosophical methods, and the method must be suited in every case to the material to which it is applied. We should not expect problems about pain to yield to the same measures as problems about thinking.

Preface

I am supposing throughout these inquiries that in Wittgenstein's view there is just one aim, that of showing that our difficulty arises through taking a problem-generating word to be of a sort different from what it actually is. But to achieve that aim, many devices may be required from case to case, and one cannot at all count on it that a point that has seemed well taken in one case will be effective as it stands in another case that may seem quite similar.

In these deliberations there will be various kinds of issue that it may be important to distinguish:

(i) whether Wittgenstein would try to clear up this or that specific difficulty in the way I propose;

(ii) whether the various ways I suggest of dealing with philosophical difficulties are specific cases of looking on words as instruments; and

(iii) whether the generality of the forms of argument I attribute to Wittgenstein, if not each and every specific instance of such a form, are in themselves sound and defensible.

It is important to understand the difference between the first and second of these kinds of question: I might for example be right about what Wittgenstein would say about intending, while being quite wrong about whether seeing intending that was is what he would offer as a specific instance seeing the verb 'to intend' as an instrument. In Part 1 I am mainly concerned with the first of these kinds of question, while in Part 2 there is an extensive review of the evidence bearing on the second kind. Not until the Epilogue is there a discussion of the soundness or defensibility of the tactics I have attributed to Wittgenstein.

On the exegetical questions that abound, there is usually not much textual evidence, and such evidence as there is is often itself greatly in need of interpretation. Hence I can make no claim that any of this is established conclusively, or even with high probability. I can only say on the one hand that I have sketched out an extensive picture of a reputable way of transacting at least some kinds of philosophical business and, on the other, that I have provided some reason to believe that this picture makes specific a good deal that Wittgenstein indicated to us about how he thought philosophy should be done, but indicated only in the form of clues that might effect the likelihood of our getting somewhere when we think about these matters for ourselves.

A number of the words I discuss I have written about elsewhere, generally at much greater length. I have included summaries of these writings partly because, when they appeared in print before, the lines I was taking were not cast as cases or ways of looking on words as instruments; partly because, as I mentioned earlier, I thought it desirable to provide a profusion of examples to bring out how different the techniques may have to be in different cases; and partly because since writing about many of these words, I think I have come to see more clearly what the problem is, and how best to resolve it.

ABBREVIATIONS

BB
The Blue and Brown Books
Basil Blackwell, Oxford 1958

PI
Philosophical Investigations
third edition
The Macmillan Co., New York 1968

PG
Philosophical Grammar
Basil Blackwell, Oxford 1978

RPP
Remarks on the Philosophy of Psychology
Basil Blackwell, Oxford 1980

Z
Zettel
Basil Blackwell, Oxford 1967

All references without attributions are to
Philosophical Investigations

Part 1

INTRODUCTION

Wittgenstein sometimes suggested looking on words as instruments, for example in the following passages from *Philosophical Investigations* (*PI*):

> 291. What we call *descriptions* are instruments for particular uses.
>
> 360. . . . Look on the word 'to think' as a tool.
>
> 421. . . . But does it worry you if I say 'These three struts give the building stability'? Are three and stability tangible? – Look at the sentence as an instrument, and its sense as its employment.
>
> 492. To invent a language could mean to invent an instrument for a particular purpose in accordance with the laws of nature, (or consistently with them); but it also has the other sense analogous to that in which we speak of the invention of a game.
>
> 569. Language is an instrument. Its concepts are instruments.

In other passages, tables, rules and paradigms are described as tools, instruments and expedients.

In their contexts, some of these remarks seem intended to be of the first importance, but Wittgenstein was never helpful about what he meant by them. It is not explained how one is supposed to go about looking on words as instruments – whether for example it is a matter of thinking about what we use them *for*, or thinking about how we manage or manipulate them, or considering how they in themselves function, or what; and it is not explained in the case of any particular word what we shall discover about it through looking on it as an instrument. Nor are there explicit indications of what sorts of philosophical dividend Wittgenstein thought would accrue from regarding them as instruments.

1

My aim is to work out answers to questions like this. I will attempt this partly by attending to the available textual clues; but since these do not, I have found, take us very far, I will also rely in part on philosophical, rather than exegetical, considerations. I will begin, for example, by looking for features of at least some words, and senses of the word 'instrument', in which it might be *true* and of some philosophical interest that a word is an instrument, or like an instrument. When such a tactic pays off, I shall have in hand something that might serve as a small part of a theory regarding what this 'words as instruments' business is all about. I would prefer to be able either to demonstrate that such a point correctly interprets Wittgenstein, or at least to show that to be highly probable, but all too often the most I shall be able to claim is that there is some evidence that I have got Wittgenstein right, and that if his point is as I suggest then, whether or not it is ultimately defensible, it is a point of some philosophical consequence.

I am primarily interested in the philosophical, rather than the exegetical. Although I do not take the fact that a proposed interpretation is philosophically interesting as evidence for its truth, still if I have succeeded in extracting some philosophical sense from a difficult stretch of Wittgenstein's prose, I will have achieved some of what I am always seeking; and when I do come away with something of apparent philosophical value, then if it turns out that this is not the point Wittgenstein intended, I will at least be glad of the dividend that my methods of unscrambling him have yielded.

There are some initial points about the key passages that should be noted, that have some tendency to affect the probability that this or that interpretation is right.

1. In the main texts I have quoted and referred to, the words tool and instrument are translations in various cases of four different German words: '*Werkzeug*', a word used mostly for such articles as hammers, saws and pickaxes, '*Instrument*', a word used in much the same way as its English counterpart, to refer to such various objects as scalpels, ammeters, violins and some legal documents, '*Mittel*', meaning a means or an expedient, and '*Vorrichtung*', which means appliance, contrivance or mechanism. Most often '*Werkzeug*' is translated 'tool', but in §360, where the German has '*Instrument*', the English has 'tool'. The similar English expressions 'the instruments of language' and 'an instrument of our language', which

appear in §§ 16 and 57 respectively, have 'instrument' as the translation of *'Werkzeug'* in §16, and of *'Mittel'* in §57. *'Mittel'* and *'Vorrichtung'* are always translated 'instrument'.

These words do not themselves provide any clear indication what, if anything, we should regard as a paradigmatic instrument for this purpose, and it could make an important difference what we decide about that. If hammers and scalpels were taken as model instruments, that would provide some reason to suppose that the emphasis was either on the fact that (or the way that) we manage them, or (more likely) on what we achieve through our management of them; but if barometers or ammeters were models, then since we do not in the same way wield them, and do not use them to produce effects, the emphasis might more likely be on the design features that make them function the way they do.

While it might make little difference whether words and so on were being likened to hammers, which are not generally called instruments, or to scalpels, which often are, it might make a lot of difference whether the comparison was with scalpels, ammeters or deeds of land. While on any of these suppositions Wittgenstein still *might* have had in mind anything with which something is done, and the emphasis then would be on what was done, rather than on what did it, if instruments (like barometers) that are mechanisms were the model, the emphasis might be less on what we do with them than on how they work. This reading would be strongly indicated if *'Vorrichtung'* had been used throughout.

2. Many interpreters of Wittgenstein seem to assume without question that he had in mind scalpels, hammers and pliers as prime examples of instruments. This inclines them to suppose that the point of the instrument analogy is to get us to focus on the purposes served by our uses of words. But there is no better reason for this interpretation than the free translation of the German *'Instrument'* as 'tool' in §360.

3. In §14, where Wittgenstein likens words to the tools in a toolbox, it is likely, but not because of the different words used in German, that he was making a quite different point from that in §360, where he suggested looking on the verb 'to think' as a tool (*Instrument*). In §14 he suggested that just as it would be a mistake to expect that all the items in a toolbox would have something in common, simply because they are all called tools, so it would be a mistake to look for what is

common to all words. (His point here is not well crafted: he uses rulers, glue pots and nails as counterexamples to the imagined thesis that all tools are used to modify something, but we do not call any of these tools, although they may be standard items in some toolboxes.) For the purpose of the point that words need have nothing in common, the analogy of tools is no better than any example where we might wrongly expect that everything bearing the same name would have common properties. In § 360, whatever Wittgenstein is up to, he is not making that point. He is talking only about one word, not about words generally, and here other analogies would presumably not do just as well as that of tools (or instruments, if there is a difference).

4. It is not always clear whether Wittgenstein meant to say that *some* words are instruments, or that they all are. His view might have been that, when in philosophical difficulty, it is always worth considering whether a troublesome word might be an instrument (whatever that might mean). When he recommends looking on the verb 'to think' as an instrument, he may be suggesting that it, unlike some other words, can be so regarded. It is not only not easy to find a way in which every and any word can be thought of as an instrument, it is unlike Wittgenstein to make such a sweeping statement. On the other hand there is nothing very guarded or qualified about the statement in §569 that 'Language is an instrument. Its concepts are instruments.' If we take this pronouncement seriously, it will be very difficult to suggest an interpretation sufficiently commodious to apply plausibly to words in general, rather than just to some large or small class of words. The interpretation I shall be proposing is sufficiently commodious, I believe.

5. §492 is perhaps unfortunate in that it could well be read as a rejection of the idea that words can be thought of as instruments. Wittgenstein says we *could* think of inventing a language as inventing an instrument for a particular purpose, but he almost certainly thought this would be a mistake, and preferred an analogy with inventing a game. Since games can hardly be thought of as instruments, he would appear to be getting away here with from the view that words are instruments. However the point is probably not that inventing a language would not be inventing an instrument, but that it would not be a *particular kind* of instrument – one designed

in accordance with laws of nature to serve a purpose specified in advance. We do not have a desire to checkmate, and invent chess as a means of satisfying it, but we invent chess and in so doing create the possibility of acquiring a taste for checkmating. Or again we do not have a desire for a way of making people move closer, and experiment with sounds until we find that the sound 'come' had that effect, and henceforth use it as our instrument for this purpose (cf. §493). But that is not to say that the word 'come' is not an instrument, just not that kind of instrument.

The point here has some tendency to discredit the idea that tools should be taken here as model instruments, since it is generally true of tools that they are invented in accordance with the laws of nature to serve a purpose of ours independently of their invention.

I am inclined to take part of the point of this passage to be that the explanation of the survival of a language would be like the explanation of the survival of a game: not that it served a purpose, but that it suited human beings.

6. Legal instruments are the only kind that are actually composed of words and sentences, and might for that reason be regarded as a particularly promising model for an interpretation.

7. Since it is a general truth about instruments of whatever kind that they are used for something, Wittgenstein might merely have been suggesting that we always consider what a word is used for. If so there would be no further problem about what he meant in these passages, even if there were a host of problems about what we use this and that word for; but we would have those problems anyway. It is clear at large that he did think it important sometimes to consider what a word is used for; but, if that were all he wanted to say in our problem passages, it is hard to see what purpose would be served by saying it so very obliquely.

I am sceptical about whether the question what we use words for is the burden of these remarks about words and so on being regarded as instruments, and I will explain why that interpretation seems to me doubtful. The considerations I will adduce are mainly philosophical, rather than textual.

Is every kind of instrument used for something? If so, do they all serve a purpose in the same sense? We can say that we use scalpels to make incisions, thermometers to register temperature, violins to play violin music, and deeds of land to transfer ownership, but there are various differences:

(i) We *wield* scalpels and violins to produce their effects, but not ammeters or deeds of land. And it is not clear whether we wield words, except perhaps in special cases. 'What's your name?', when suitably 'wielded', can be quite sexy, but it is not usually so.

(ii) There is a causal relation between the wielding of scalpels or violins, and the achievement of the purposes for which they are wielded, but it is at the very least a dark saying that thermometers cause us to know what the temperature is; and the relation between deeds of land and changes of ownership is not causal [see argument in '(iii)' below); nor do words like 'Leave the room' cause us to get up and go (see below, p. 7).

(iii) We could have a job we wanted done, and design a chisel or a scalpel to do it, but it is not so clear whether, with other kinds of instrument, including words, we could specify the task before having the instrument with which to do it. We didn't want violin music and design the violin to produce it, rather we gradually refined violin designs until we liked the sound produced, and we did not know what sound that would be until it was produced.

We didn't tinker with documents until we got one that would do the job of transferring ownership, didn't try various wordings, thicknesses of paper and what not, until we got one that worked. Lawyers have indeed tinkered with the wordings of deeds, but not with a view to finding one that reliably caused a change of ownership, as they might if the owners of property were registered in the heavens, and only the proper incantation would change what the heavenly registry office showed. The job done by a deed is spelled out in the document, and is not an effect of signing it, but is done in signing it.

Might the fact that a word would serve a certain purpose have been a discovery? Language, one might think, could have started when some observant person noticed that when she made the sound that we now write as 'come', people moved closer, and when she made the sound 'go', they moved further off. She might then have tried out all the distinctly different sounds she could think of and watched for regularities in what then happened, and so discovered that, when she made the sound 'dog', people looked at dogs, and on the sound 'every dog' being produced, they went around to all the dogs, and so on. It might just have happened that in England things worked this way, while in France those sounds either had a different effect or none, and Frenchmen visiting England and seeing what the English were doing with noises had to experiment when they got home until they discovered the effect of 'venez', 'allez', and 'chien'.

But clearly even if some rudimentary discoveries of that kind had been made, a language such as ours could not have been constructed just out of sequences of those sounds. It is not just that it is improbable that there would be a sufficient array of natural reactions to sounds to make possible our use of words such as 'wish', 'understand' and 'believe'. We can see how improbable it would be that even such a simple request as 'Come later' should in the way suggested acquire the sense it has for us. The sound 'come' might make people approach, and the sound 'later' might set them to pointing at people who are sleeping in and to pairs of actions that are performed in sequence, like cooking and eating, but to assure that 'Come later' would get people to come, but not right away, rather than to come and then go around pointing at late risers, one might have to discourage the latter behaviour, and perhaps play-act someone twiddling his thumbs for a bit and then coming. And, if one could carry this off, one could do it as well, if not better, if the sounds 'come' and 'later' begot no natural reaction.

[Wittgenstein makes similar points in *PI* §§492–8. In §492, as we have seen, he says 'To invent a language could mean to invent an instrument for a particular purpose on the basis of the laws of nature (or consistently with them)', and in § 493 he says we might imagine that a cock's crowing sets the hens in motion by a kind of physical causation, or that the words 'Come to me' act on a person in such a way that finally the muscles of his legs are innervated. But clearly he dismisses these suppositions. In §496 he says that Grammar does not tell us how language must be constructed in order ... to have such and such an effect on human beings'; and in §498 he argues that although the words 'Milk me sugar' may make a person stare and gape, and although that may be just the effect desired, those words do not therefore mean 'stare and gape'. ('Milk me sugar' might for all that be an instrument, but the interesting thing would be how it worked: not the way I imagined 'come' and 'go' working, but in a way relying on our general grasp of English and our consequent inability to understand the sentence 'Milk me sugar'.)]

(iv) Speaking of the way a word is used would be an inept way of talking about what it is used for, just as a description of how a hammer is used ('You swing it thus') is distinct from an account of what it is used for ('To sink nails').

(v) It will by no means always be illuminating to know what we use a word (an expression, a sentence) for. We use 'I am wiggling my toes' to report the wiggling of toes, and 'it's a fine winter's day' to say what kind of day it is. These observations seem extremely obvious and unimportant.

The foregoing provides some reason to think, first that the point of the proposal that we look on words as instruments was not to get us thinking about what we use them for; and secondly that instruments like deeds, violins and thermometers, which in the sense indicated create the job they do, may be more apt models than hammers or scalpels, where the concept of the job to be done pre-exists the tool, and the tool is devised in accordance with the laws of nature (or consistently with them).

The two most obvious interpretive possibilities that remain are that we are meant to think of how we manage or wield words, on the analogy of the way we play a violin or swing a hammer, and that we in intended to think in some way about the instruments themselves – of something corresponding to the design of a jigsaw, a barometer or a flute.

I will consider briefly the remote possibility that we are meant to consider the way we manage or manipulate words, on the analogy of the way we swing a hammer, twist a screwdriver or push a plane. I suppose we do in a sense exercise skills in the handling of words, in the differences of emphasis or intonation that express tentativeness or show that we are asking a question rather than making a request, and so on; but I can neither think of a way in which this fact is likely to be of major philosophical importance, nor suggest how bearing it in mind might help us over our difficulties in any of the contexts in which Wittgenstein recommends looking on words as instruments.

Turning to the remaining initially plausible line of interpretation, there would be a way of thinking about the words themselves, rather than about what they are used for, if there was something intricate, or not what one might have expected, about the ways they functioned. ('You see how when you push here, it turns there. From this you can see what it can be used for, – driving screws and drilling holes but not sinking nails.') Here we both see a connection, and also a difference, between the instrument and what it is used for, but the primary interest is in the way it works, in the design features that enable it to do its job.

In other cases a different kind of interest in the instrument might be taken. For example it might be noted that while a barometer is designed in such a way as to show atmospheric pressure, and a clock in such a way as to tell time, a barometer's mechanism is registering changes in its current environment, whereas a clock's is not. When a timepiece says five o'clock it has not *detected* the time, and when it shows that an hour has passed, it is not as if it had measured the length of time that had run through it, the way a device for selling rope will tell you when 10 metres of it have run through.

If, analogously, words, sentences and so on work in various ways – if there can be two sentences that do the same job, but do it in different ways, and if it is of some interest what these differences are – the invitation to look on words as instruments might be an encouragement to consider, not so much the job they do, as how they do it. To take an uninteresting example, 'The number of coins in my pocket is equal to the square root of 49' and 'The number of coins in my pocket is equal to the number of planets in the solar system' say the same, but, while in one case we are required to count, in the other we are required to calculate or know the square root of 49. We could say these sentences were different instruments, and saying this would be pointing to differences, not in what they do, but in how they do it.

Most of the foregoing observations tend to weigh against various interpretive hypotheses, and there is little that gives a strong positive indication about what Wittgenstein might have meant. It appears to me therefore that we are in the position of having to act on a hunch – take a leap beyond anything for which there is strong supporting evidence. When, pursuant to the hypothesis we then posit, we have worked out in some detail its consequences for a representative array of philosophical difficulties, and also explored how far we get good sense when we feed it into the contexts in which looking on words as instruments is recommended, we shall have provided as strong a verification of the hypothesis as can be hoped for.

The thesis I will defend is that looking on words as instruments is a matter of taking an interest in the ways they function, in a sense analogous to that in which we can study how a violin, a barometer or a pair of pliers functions.

What I mean by this I hope to make clear enough in the various sorts of example that follow.

HOW SOME WORDS WORK

I wish now to distinguish eight different kinds of way in which words might be said to 'work', in a sense like that in which barometers, tubas and timepieces work. In each case I shall give a number of examples. In distinguishing only eight kinds, I do not mean to imply that there are no others. If there are more, I doubt if the total comes to hundreds, or even nineteen, but that might depend on how far we made small differences a basis for adding to the number of types. Eight types in any case should be enough to show that skill and care will be important in these matters, and that we shall by no means always be able to diagnose our perplexity in the same way – saying for example that it has arisen through not doubting that a problem word stands for an object (or a quality, or an action).

Just as an instrument may be partly mechanical, partly electronic, or may function partly in such a way as to monitor current conditions, partly by containing a time-registering device, so a word may exemplify more than one of the patterns I shall be describing, and hence may be discussed in more than one place.

I assume that the use of some words will include many tangled strands. I will not be attempting to map out the whole of the mish-mash in any particular case, but only some selected features.

The following then are some of the ways words work:

1.1 Performatives

Whereas to say 'I am wiggling my toes' is not itself to wiggle them, to say 'I promise' is to promise. We are not reporting promising, but doing it, in saying 'I promise', and the same is true for a large number of other words, in the first person present indicative, including 'order, 'guarantee', 'assure', 'vow', 'disavow', 'renounce', 'confess', 'accept', 'decline', 'propose', 'suggest', 'offer', 'give', 'donate', 'affirm', 'deny', 'retract', 'object', 'declare', 'announce', 'invite', 'choose' and 'recognize'.

I will call words that work this way 'performatives'.

Some salient features of performatives are;

(i) Although we do not always precede these verbs with the word 'hereby', in the first person singular present tense it is always allowable to do so, in a way that is not allowable with for example the word 'believe'.

(ii) In using them in the first person singular present indicative, we are performing an act describable using the same verb in another person or tense.

(iii) Significance of various kinds is conventionally attached to the performance of these acts. By performing them we make a commitment, take a stand, make it official, and so on. We get ourselves into something of some consequence or, as I shall often say, 'take the plunge'.

(iv) Whether to take the step of using a particular performative verb in this way is a strategic question, a question of the advantages and disadvantages of putting ourselves in the position into which this speech act will set us.

(v) To be held to the consequences conventionally attaching to the performance of the act, it is enough to have uttered the words in appropriate circumstances. For example, in normal circumstances it is just my having said 'I promise to pay you on Tuesday' that commits me to doing this, and having had no intention to do it is not an argument that I did not promise or am not committed.

Whereas I shall have much to say in what follows about other ways in which various words and expressions work, I shall take it that the concept of a performative is familiar enough by now, that the foregoing account of their workings may suffice.

There are various ways in which recognizing that a word is performative may resolve a philosophical difficulty. If we are perplexed about what choosing is, that is, about what the words 'I choose' report, the answer will be that they do not report anything that one is not reporting choosing, but doing it, in saying those words.

It is worth noting also how very many words are performative: not just 'promise', 'order', 'guarantee' and 'christen', but at least all the words listed above.

1.2 Quasi-performatives

Some words, although unlike performatives in that using them is not performing an act describable using the same word in the second or third person, can be seen as being *performative-like* if they are so translatable as to show that in using them in the first person present tense we are doing something rather than reporting the *doing* of something. One promises by saying 'I promise', but does not believe by saying 'I believe'; yet 'I believe *P*' can be translated 'I assert *P* although I recognize that its truth is debatable'; and 'assert' and 'recognize' are performative verbs.

The following are some of the words that are quasi-performative.

2.2.1 'Intend'

It may seem as if, that one is intending to do such and such, is something one reports about oneself, something other people would at most suspect if one did not tell them, but of which one is oneself aware, in the way in which one may be aware of a pain or an itch. The intending, we are apt to suppose, need not be something of which one is aware concurrently with saying one intends. It might be a tendency one has, for example to have certain feelings when one entertains a certain plan of action, so that, just as it can be true at times when I am not smoking that I smoke a pipe, it may be true that I am intending to go to the meeting at times when the phenomenon of intending, whatever it may be, is not occurring. [Here I had to go out of my way not to say ' . . . at times when I am not so intending', which would have parallelled '... at times when I am not smoking'. If one smokes a pipe, there are times when one is engaged in smoking it, but if I am intending to go to Honey Harbour, are there times when I am engaged in so intending?]

Yet, if, in saying we intend thus and so, we are recording something about ourselves, it seems both very hard to say what it is, and surprising that we should not know, and should have to cast around for, an answer to that question.

There are many things that typically happen when we are intending, but we do not call any of them intending, and there seems nothing else that we do so describe. We may feel excited or anxious when we think about what we are intending to do. We may make preparations for doing it, and may seek the advice of friends about it, or just chatter a lot about it. But we do not say 'I did a lot of intending to buy a spinnaker today. I thought about what colours I'd like, and read advertisements and visited shops and asked every sailing friend I met for advice.

We do not figure that intending lapses, or continues unabated either, when for a while we are totally pre-occupied with other things, or sound asleep; and while we may be inclined to assume that, whether we are aware of it or not, there must be something that does not change the whole time we have a given intention, we have not the least idea what this is, and it is not on the basis of knowing it to prevail that we say we are intending thus and so.

We do in some ways talk as if intending were something that occurred at (fairly) definite times We say for example 'When I said that, I was intending to invite George', or 'All week I have been intending to phone him when I get a chance'. Here it may sound as if intending were going on alongside of other things we were doing (cf. 'When I said that, I was looking in his direction'); but we may begin to see that intending is not a concurrent process when we reflect that, while we can alternatively say '*As* I said that, I was looking in his direction', we would not know what to make of someone saying 'As I said that, I was intending to invite George.'

If we have had an intention all week, we cannot have had it continuously or unremittingly, in the way that anxiety or pain might be continuous or unremitting (cf. *PI* §148). To say that we have been vacillating about doing something does not mean that intending has been occurring and then letting up for a time, the way perhaps our excitement over what we are intending may come in spurts. And it does not mean that intending x has been occurring, interspersed with intending not-x.

We could float clear of all this perplexity about what 'I intend . . . ' records if we supposed that the trouble derives from the fact that those words do not record anything, that professing an intention is not that kind of speech act. If it were the quasi-performative act of issuing a kind of restricted entitlement to count on our doing the thing we say we intend, our question what it reports would not arise, and would not require an answer.

What is another person entitled to expect, if I say I intend to go to the meeting? Something like this: 'Don't expect me to go if I am too tired, or if something important comes up but, failing anything like that, you can count on it.' This is of course vague, but these things just *are* vague.

If various kinds of right to expect us to do something were well known, and marked by expressions such as 'an *i*-entitlement' and 'a *p*-entitlement', 'I intend to do such and such' would be like 'I authorize an *i*-entitlement to expect me to do it', and would thereby be shown to have a quasi-performative character.

'Intend' is one of various words we use to issue entitlements of this kind, each entitlement having a somewhat different character. We can get some feel for the character of that issued by the word 'intend' if we compare saying we intend with saying we promise, we plan and we propose.

'I promise' makes a moral commitment such that we may be expected to overcome quite serious obstacles in order to act as we promised, and few excuses will be allowable as of right.

There is no such strong moral commitment attaching to the words 'intend', 'plan' or 'propose'. The latter words leave us at liberty morally not to perform, but may give another person such a right as to be forewarned if we change our minds.

If I say 'I am planning to go', there is a suggestion, derived from the idea of a plan, and not necessarily from any actual plan I have, that, if I do not go, it will be in accordance with a rational strategy, such as might have been plotted in advance, for example that I will go if A and B occur, but not if they do not, and not if C occurs. It is like saying 'You may count on my doing it unless, in the circumstances then prevailing, my not doing it is the kind of thing I might well have planned on.'

To say 'I am proposing to go' similarly authorizes an expectation, but by also indicating preparedness to discuss whether to go, suggests uncertainty about the merits of going. It is like saying that if I do not go it will be because I have been dissuaded, not for example because I didn't feel like it.

'I intend' might also be compared usefully with 'I am quite inclined', or 'I am very likely do it'. Whereas in all three cases a doubt will remain about whether one will in fact do the contemplated action, 'intend' does actually issue a qualified entitlement, while the other locutions stop short of doing so.

How do we know in which of these ways to express ourselves? It may seem right to reply 'Say you intend if you do intend', or 'Say it is settled with qualifications if it is so settled', but if there is nothing we call intending and nothing we call settling with qualifications, this advice can only mean 'Say you are intending if you can accept the expectations that will be generated by your so expressing yourself.' To decide that question one thinks, not about oneself, but about strategy: about what one will be getting into if one takes the step of authorizing this expectation.

What difference will it make which way I express myself? In some cases if I have said only that I am quite inclined, and subsequently perform the action in question, there may be complaints that I did it without adequate forewarning, complaints that could not arise if I had said I was intending to do it; and on the other side of the coin if I do not do something I said I was intending to do, there may be complaints, that could not have arisen if I had only said I was quite inclined to do it. We say we are intending to do something, not if on examining ourselves we find so intending going on, and not if it is so obviously going on that we do not need to examine ourselves, but if we want to avoid complaints of not having given adequate forewarning, and if we are prepared to have another people counting on our doing it to the extent that our so expressing ourselves warrants their doing. Here we are not thinking about our present state, but about the advantages and disadvantages of performing a particular speech act, given which something will be expected of us.

There is another aspect of the use of 'intend' where we can see ourselves as doing something with the word, rather than reporting something. This may be called the independence feature. If I am in a position to order someone to do something, or if it is clear that it is important to me whether he does it, but I wish to put it that it is up to him whether he does it (that he should not do it to oblige me) I may, rather than urging him to do it, or ordering him to do it, ask him whether he intends to do it. My use of the word 'intend' declares it to be up to him what he does, *grants* him independence. In a similar way if I have begged someone to do something and she wishes to indicate that she is going to do it, but for her own reasons and not to please me, she may say she is intending to do it, rather than for example 'All right, I'll do it.' Here by using the word 'intend' she *stakes out* her independence.

If we ask 'Do you intend . . .?', we are not inquiring about the existence of an intention, but rather saying 'It's up to you, but what is it to be?' Similarly if one says 'Well I don't care. I intend to do thus and so', one is not reporting the existence or the persistence of an intention, and not saying that one is an independent sort, but *being* independent. Expressing oneself this way is a (mildly) defiant act, more like shaking a fist than like reporting a feeling of independence.

These again are not performative speech acts. There is no place for the word 'hereby', and one does not intend by saying 'I intend'. Indeed intending is not an act at all, and could not be performed in this or any other way. But there is an act we are performing, the act (in the first person) of staking out or declaring independence, or (in the second person) of recognizing or allowing another person's independence.

Just as there are conditions in which we see fit to make a promise or to make an order official, so there are conditions in which we stake out or recognize independence. These are generally strategic or diplomatic considerations. We perceive for example that we may be able to wrap up some inconclusive negotiations by taking a stand for our own part. But just as in making a promise we are not talking about the considerations that led us to make it, and the promise is made whatever those considerations may have been, so we are not talking about why we saw fit to go our own way in saying 'Well, I intend thus and so', but doing it; and we have made a gesture of independence if we say this, no matter what our reasons may have been.

There is not much evidence on whether Wittgenstein would subscribe to any of this; but consider PI § 247:

> 'Only you can know if you had that intention.' One might tell someone this when one was explaining the meaning of the word 'intention' to him. For then it means that is how we use it.
>
> (And here 'know' means that the expression of uncertainty is senseless.)

This last is a confusing remark, partly because at *PI* p. 223 Wittgenstein says that 'He alone can know what he intends' is nonsense. But in a large number of places, Wittgenstein seems to take the view that grammatical points when not marked as

16

such are nonsense if they sound like empirical generaliza-
tions, but not if their grammatical character is well understood.
'Only he can know . . .' sounds like 'Only he has access . . .',
and Wittgenstein would call this nonsense. But it is not
nonsense if taken as a way of saying that we ask *him* (and may
not *tell* him) what his intention is. That is part of the way we
use this word. (Compare p. 224: '"He.alone knows his motives" – that is an expression of the fact that we ask *him* what
his motives are.')

Why can we not tell him what his intention is? Wittgenstein
does not say, but it would be an answer to say 'Because
"intend" is used to express independence, and no one else can
do this for us', or [in other uses] 'Because "intend" authorizes
entitlements, and these authorizations can be issued only by
the person who will be expected to do something'.

If Wittgenstein takes it to be clear that we ask him and may
not tell him what his intention is, and if the explanation of this
is not that intentions are private, the preceding paragraph
would provide an alternative; and what other explanation
might there be?

1.2.2 'Believe'

'I believe . . ' seems to say something about me. The hard
question is, what? That whenever I am asked whether the
proposition I say I believe is true, I say yes? That whenever I
ask myself whether it is true, the answer 'Yes' comes? That
when I entertain the proposition, I have a feeling of conviction? That I act (or will or would under certain circumstances
act) as if the proposition were true (or as a person with my aims
and purposes would be well advised to act if the proposition
were true)? That with respect to this proposition I am given to
performing the indescribable mental act we have all come to
call believing? That my mental picture of the state of affairs
described by the proposition has a vividness and steadiness
approaching that of actually experiencing such a state of
affairs?

There are well-known and convincing objections to all
such answers, and it should not be necessary to review them
in detail, but some of the more central difficulties might be
mentioned.

One may believe what one has only now heard or read, and
this rules out references to past performance, at least if offered

as a perfectly general account of believing. If you tell me something and I believe it, I may still believe it years later, although I have not thought of it once in the intervening time, and this rules out answers referring to tendencies or recurrent responses, at least as a general account of past believing. I believe much of what I read in respectable newspapers, but nothing in particular happens: no feelings of conviction, no asking myself 'Is this true?' and having the answer 'Yes' come back, no vivid picturing of the scene described, or no more vivid picturing than may occur if I am reading a novel, and so on.

What kind of word is 'believe' then? Saying one believes something is (in part) saying it is true, and if we ask what kind of speech act this is, the first point to be noted is that 'Such and such is true' does not say anything about me, and hence there is no longer a question of *what* 'I believe' says about me.

We shall of course often have reasons for saying something is true, and that I have such and such reasons may be a fact about me; but saying one believes such and such is not saying one has reasons for it; and, except in the special case in which the proposition believed is about ourselves, the reasons ought not to include any facts about the speaker, but will rather be for example that there is plenty of evidence for it, that the sources of information about it are reliable, that there is no reason to suspect chicanery, and so on. One *can* work in references to oneself here: what I have seen, what I have read, the fact that it was told me by so and so, the fact that I have never heard anyone question it, and so on; but all these references are eliminable. If I say so and so told me and I have always found him reliable, that can be re-written 'So and so said it, and he is reliable.' Of course the information that he said it and that he is reliable will have reached me, but its having reached me is not part of my reason for saying that what he said is true. I do not have three reasons, that he said it and is reliable and that these facts have reached me. The first two are enough. Circumstances are perhaps imaginable in which the fact that something reached me might be significant, for example if my informant surely would not lie to *me*, of all people, but this case is no more significant than that in which he told Sarah, and he would surely not lie to her.

Whatever our reasons for believing something, the act we perform in saying we believe it is that of affirming its truth, taking a stand about its truth. We will sometimes be deciding about its truth *in* saying we believe it, but more generally when a question arises about whether we believe something, it will be something we have believed for some time, and we will not re-open the question whether it is true, or review our reasons for believing it. Even so we are not *saying* we have believed it for some time, that yesterday or last week we would also have said it is true. The present speech act does not record past affirmations, or the longstanding fact that we would have so affirmed if the occasion had arisen, but is another in the series of affirmations.

Since in the most typical case we do not at all think about whether the proposition we affirm is true, but just routinely affirm it, it is natural to suppose that something about us, some acquired state of the nervous system perhaps, makes us say 'Yes' when asked 'Is such and such true?'; but whether or not such a state of the nervous system exists, we are not adverting to it in saying we believe something, any more than a calculator is adverting to its design in saying $25^2=625$.

It is sometimes suggested that we use the word 'believe' when we are uncertain whether a proposition is true, as if we were saying we suspect it is true, think it is probably true, or partly true, or would not be prepared to bet much on its truth, but might bet a little. But if we only suspect, think probably true or partly true, that is what we should have said; and how much we are prepared to bet on it is independent of whether we believe it. 'I believe it and would bet my life on it' is not at all odd. In saying we believe something we are flat out declaring it to be true.

The supposition that 'believe' expresses some doubt about the proposition believed may lead to supposing that, in saying we believe, we are recording a state of uncertainty – that is what we are saying about ourselves, alongside of what we say about the proposition believed. Yet it would be very odd to say 'This is true and I am uncertain whether it is.' We sometimes have occasion to say something quite *like* this: 'I am uncertain, but if I had to say yes or no to the question whether it is true, I would say yes'; but this is a special case, and not what we are taken to be saying when we simply say we believe something.

If I say I believe that Sarah is living in Vancouver now, I may be mindful of the possibility that she has moved again since last I heard, but I am not saying that this or any other such possibility has left me in actual doubt and, if I *am* in doubt, I ought not to say I believe. In saying we believe we are not saying we are certain, but if we are uncertain we mis-speak if we say we believe, and would be better to say we suspect or are inclined to believe.

Does one not have to be either certain or uncertain? If one is not uncertain, does it follow that one is certain? No. If I read in a newspaper that Peter Martin, aged 23, was arrested and charged with being in possession of burglar's tools, I will generally have no reason to doubt it, and so will not be uncertain, but if I am asked 'Are you certain then?', I may say 'Of course not. All I know about it is what it says here, and for all I know there might be a misprint here or a case of mistaken identity; or it might be a prank. I would have to know more than I do in order to be certain, but the fact that the story might be misleading in all kinds of ways does not induce me to suspect that it *is* misleading, and so I can't say I am *un*certain either.'

Many religious believers are altogether certain, and yet they are called and call themselves believers. This shows that uncertainty is not implied by the use of the word 'believe'; and the fact that it is not a truism to say 'This believer is certain' shows that certainty is not implied either.

Why then does this question of uncertainty arise at all? Why does it seem at all right to connect professions or attributions of belief with uncertainty? There is a confusion between being uncertain and recognizing there is room for uncertainty.

We recognize room for uncertainty when the evidence, however impressive, is not conclusive, or when it is possible that what has been taken to be evidence has been faked or misunderstood, or when it is not very clear what would count as evidence; but on most questions no one demands that the evidence should be conclusive, and most of us require more than just a general possibility of fakery or misunderstanding, to throw us into actual doubt.

To say one believes something is to say (a) that it is true, and (b) that one recognizes room for doubt about it. The latter, at least when expressed that way, seems to say something about oneself, but we can readily see this to be an illusion. In the first place, the recognition might be written 'I acknowledge that there is room for uncertainty', and then it would be a clear performative, and in the second place the recognition of room for doubt is not about oneself but about the epistemological status of the proposition said to be true – that the evidence for it is inconclusive, or that it is not impossible that it should have been faked, etc. A computer designed to use weather reports from stations around the globe as a basis for weather predictions in a given locality, and designed (a) to answer only 'yes' or 'no' to questions such as 'Will it rain in the next four hours?' or 'Will the winds be north-westerly?', and (b) where the evidence is inconclusive, to preface its answer with the words 'I believe', would clearly, in saying that it 'believed', not be saying anything about itself, but only about the forthcoming weather and about the status of its prediction.

'Believe' is not a performative word, but in saying we believe a proposition we perform the joint act of declaring it true and recognizing that there is room for doubt regarding its truth – performative acts both.

If we say 'I believed it', however, we are not saying we *declared* it true and recognized room for doubt. Very often no declaration will have been made, and it might be that at the time referred to one did not in fact recognize room for doubt. We could say however that 'I believed' means in part that at the time I *would have* declared it true; and that here the recognition of room-for-doubt aspect works out differently in different cases. When we say 'I believed it and still do', the present recognition of room for doubt carries over into the past; but if we say 'I believed it and am no longer so sure', we may be using 'believe' in present expression of a doubtfulness we did not then appreciate. It is wrong to say 'I believe it but it is not true', but allowable to say 'I believed it but it is not true'. This is an offshoot of the 'room for doubt' aspect. If there is room for doubt about a proposition, it is possible that it is false. Hence it has come to be permissible to attribute belief to other persons or to ourselves in the past when they do not or we did not have any doubt, but we are now in some doubt. Just as 'She believes' is used when I have doubts about the truth of the proposition to which she subscribes, so also 'I believed' may be used when I now have doubts about the truth of a proposition I formerly took to be undeniable.

My main point about how the word 'believe' works then – what kind of instrument it is – is that in the first person present tense it is quasi-performative. In other persons and tenses it is not performative at all, but part of the way it then works is that it says of someone else or of ourselves in the past that they would have declared a certain proposition true, while often expressing the *speaker's* present reluctance to take the same stand.

In *PI* ıı x, Wittgenstein makes various remarks that can be read as supporting what I have suggested here. He says for example:

> How did we ever come to use such an expression as 'I believe . . .'? Did we at some time become aware of a phenomenon (of belief)?

He does not answer this question, but it is almost certain that his answer would be negative.

I suggested that to say one believes *P* is in part to assert *P*, and Wittgenstein says

> . . . the statement 'I believe it's going to rain' has a meaning like, that is to say a use like, 'It's going to rain' . . .

I said we cannot say 'I am uncertain whether P is true, but I believe it', and he says

> One can mistrust one's own senses, but not one's own belief.

I presume that by this he does not mean either that we cannot reconsider the truth of a proposition, having once accepted it, or that we cannot say 'I believe it although I know it may not be true', but rather than we cannot in the same breath say 'I believe it' and 'I doubt if it is true'. (Why do I so presume? Because the points that I say he is not making are too obviously false, while the point I say he is making is both true and consistent with what he did say.)

I said that Wittgenstein did not answer the question whether we came to use the word 'believe' through becoming aware of a phenomenon of belief, but an answer may be derived from the following remarks:

> . . . 'I believe it's raining and my belief is reliable, so I have confidence in it.' – In that case my belief would be a kind of sense-impression.

I take it that he thinks the sentence in inverted commas here is nonsense, but would make sense if believing were for example having a Humean lively idea. Then from an accumulation of cases in which events turned out to resemble the lively idea we had been having, we might come to regard our lively ideas as reliable indicators of how things would be; and then it would make sense to say we trusted our belief.

1.2.3 'Know'

'Know' is not a performative verb. One does not say 'I hereby know' and, by saying 'I know', one does not perform the act of knowing. There is no such act. One can be engaged in promising, and engaged in trying to find out, but not in knowing.

It may nevertheless be performative-*like*, in the sense that in using it, or in using it in some contexts, we are not reporting, but doing something.

The most plausible line of cases in which something like that might be true is what is often called emphatic uses, as in 'I don't just believe this, I *know* it', 'Do you *know* that, or is it just hearsay?', 'I know that my Redeemer liveth', and so on.

In speaking in such ways, we might be, and are often thought to be, alleging that we have imposing grounds. That would make these uses more report-like than act-like. While alleging is an act, what would be alleged in these cases would be the existence of a state of affairs.

A difficulty would then be that one can have extremely imposing grounds, and still only describe oneself, or be describable, as believing. We would seem to need some way of marking off the imposing grounds that do, from those that do not warrant the use of 'know'.

An inviting hypothesis is that it is when we have conclusive reasons that we can rightly say we know. We surely know, if we are in command of conclusive reasons. However we can think our reasons are conclusive when they are not, and we can be in command of conclusive reasons and not draw the conclusion they warrant, and hence not say we know. We are at least partly taking a stand concerning the truth of that conclusion when we say we know.

Having conclusive reasons, or thinking one has, may be an occasion for saying one knows, but it does not follow from this that, in saying, we know we are saying we have conclusive reasons, just as, although believing a watch to be reliable is a good reason for guaranteeing it, it does not follow that guaranteeing it is saying it is reliable. We can reputably guarantee a watch whether we know it to be reliable or not.

Guaranteeing a watch is less risky when it is well made; and similarly one can serenely take a firm stand on the truth of a proposition one has conclusive reasons for holding to be true, but one can take a firm stand *whether or not* one has such reasons. The act of taking such a stand may be more or less madcap depending on how good one's reasons for asserting are, but 'I take a firm stand on this', or 'For me, this is not discussable', do not entail anything about my reasons.

The person who says she knows that her Redeemer liveth, or who says she just knows it will be a fine day tomorrow, does not even have *imposing* reasons, and yet it is not clear that she has misused the word 'know'. These are among the standard uses of that word; and while one may suggest to a person who talks this way that it is unwise to subscribe to a proposition of any consequence when the grounds one has for asserting it are rather slight, that is not the kind of reason we give for saying that a word has been misused.

What we are doing in saying we know in such cases is marking the proposition as one the truth of which we will not seriously discuss. So marking it is a kind of declaration we make, a dialectical action that directs how some conversational business is to be be transacted.

Most people who take this kind of stand will most often in fact have quite good reasons for doing so. They will have seen something with their own eyes, conducted inquiries or studied proofs. In most circles it will be embarrassing if one takes this stand and it turns out that one has grossly inadequate reasons; but in saying we know, we are not actually saying we have adequate or any reasons, but only for our own part declaring the proposition unshakeable. To say 'I just know…' in such cases is not incorrect English.

It may be worth dwelling on the difference between the speech act of taking a firm stand, and a possible report of a psychological disposition. One might in a reflective mood say 'I find I tend to treat this proposition as unassailable. I cringe somewhat at any suggestion that it might not be true', perhaps adding 'Isn't that curious?'. So noting would be a different affair from the act of directing other people not to expect one to doubt it. Things would run on differently. In the former case another person might ask how long this had been going on, what I thought might be causing it, and whether I thought it would soon pass. None of this would be in order in the latter case, but instead another person might avoid casting doubts on the proposition said to be known, and dwell instead on related questions.

Although the following possibility is improbable, it might sometimes be *because* the psychological report is true that someone issues the restrictive direction. The direction might be a present expression of the psychological state; but even so it would not report that the state prevailed, and would not be out of order if it did not prevail.

What I have suggested so far applies at most only to what I have called emphatic uses. What kind of instrument is 'know' in its more routine uses?

'Know' Is often used parenthetically, as for example in 'It is, I know, very important', and here for 'know' one can substitute 'agree', 'recognize', 'acknowledge' or 'concede', performative verbs all.

Another kind of case is when we ask 'Do you know Emily's phone number?', or 'Who here knows Fred's number?' Replying affirmatively is like saying 'You may ask me', an act of giving permission. One *can* ask 'Does anyone *know* Emily's number?' but, if 'know' was not used emphatically in asking the question, the questioner will not have been particularly interested in ruling out the possibility of error. We might in the same circumstances say 'Can you tell me (or can anyone here tell me) what Jenny's number is?', and then we would clearly be laying no emphasis on being right. We use 'know' here, not as a way of saying 'Answer affirmatively only if you are certain', but partly because there is no question 'Do you believe Emily's phone number?' There is a question 'Do you have a belief about what her number is?', but it is not just because that is somewhat wordy that we would not use it in the present kind of case. To use it would be to cast it as problematic what Emily's number is, and normally that would strike a false note.

In these cases we may be greatly inclined to suppose that the person who answers affirmatively is reporting having in some manner thought of the answer. She says it to herself, or pictures it as she has seen it written somewhere, or what have you. Something like this will certainly sometimes happen in such a case. We need not say this is a fiction. But nothing of that kind need happen. If you said you knew Emily's number, and I was satisfied that you had not said it to yourself, or pictured it, or anything of that sort, I could not conclude that you did not know it. It is not because I only want an answer from someone who has first said it to himself, that I ask if you know her number (rather than just asking what her number is), but because I wish to avoid the rejoinder 'Why do you ask me?' In asking whether you know, I am requesting your permission to ask you; and in replying that you do, you are giving it.

Giving permission in that way is a quasi-performative act. It is best if, when that act is performed, the person performing it can in fact go on to give a correct answer – if for example she often phones Emily, and does not have to look up her number; but it is not *on reflecting* that this happens that she may answer affirmatively; and she has performed the act of authorizing me to ask her, whether that happens or not.

If she gets it wrong, can we not object to her having said she knew? Here certainly if I had said 'Do you *know* her number?' emphasizing the importance of being right, that objection could be pressed; but it is not so clear that in the more typical case, in which there was no such emphasis, it would be appropriate to make an issue of the answer having been wrong. The person asked, let us suppose, has successfully phoned Emily dozens of times, without looking it up. That is just the kind of case in which we say 'Yes, I know it'. She was using the word quite properly. If she was wrong, someone else could say she did not know, and so could she, when she later discovered she had been wrong. But at the point in time when she said she knew, she had no special reason to suspect she might be wrong; and if a general awareness of human fallibility were treated as a reason for declining to say one knows, we could never use this word.

My question was, if she got it wrong, can we not object to her having said she knew? The reply I have given perhaps comes to this: we can note that she did not know, but we can not object that she did not. To object would imply falsely that she had misused the word – as she might if she said she knew the moon.

The foregoing are not all the uses of 'know', but only some in which the word has a quasi-performative character. Some others will be discussed in Section 1.2.

So far, without reference to Wittgenstein, I have been independently constructing a statement of a few of the ways the word 'know' works – what kind of instrument it is. There is not much evidence that Wittgenstein either actually held similar views, or might have found what I have suggested congenial, but the following passages are worth noting:

> 246. If we are using the word 'to know' as it is normally used (and how else are we to use it?), then other people very often know when I am in pain. – Yes, but not with the same certainty with which I know it myself!

Here (a) We can assume that, although on the question whether someone else is in pain there is very often room for doubt, Wittgenstein does not see this as standing in the way of our using the world 'know'; and (b) in not objecting to the expression 'to know with certainty' (but only to its application to one's relation to one's own pain), he seems to recognize that we can know without certainty, that 'to know with certainty' is not redundant.

My argument that what goes on in the mind is irrelevant is echoed in *PI* §179:

> We can also imagine the case where nothing at all occurred in B's mind except that he suddenly said 'Now I know how to go on'. . . . And in this case too we should say – in certain circumstances – that he did know how to go on.

I find nothing that supports my suggestions about the quasi-performative character of some uses of 'know', but nothing that conflicts with them either.

1.2.4 'Mean'

The discussion here will concern only those uses of 'to mean' in which *'meinen'* rather than *'bedeuten'* would be the German translation, that is, in which a person, rather than a word, is said to mean something, and in which there is a close link with that person's saying or having said something, as in 'I said it and I meant it', 'I said it, but I meant to say such and such', or 'I meant this rather than that by what 'I said.'

The surface grammar of these constructions, that is, such features as the similarity between 'I meant it' and 'I ate it', may suggest that one's meaning it or meaning such and such is something about oneself that one is recording, something that one did or felt or underwent at the time in question; and it will be natural to ask *what* it is that we are thus recording. Yet, while there are characteristic thoughts, actions and feelings that often occur at such times, we do not call these meaning it or meaning thus and so, and it is correct to use the word 'mean' even if, at the relevant time, one was not doing or undergoing anything we would be in the least tempted to call the act or process of meaning. (Indeed when you think of it, there most often is nothing of that kind going on.)

If I say Sarah will be there, and picture Sarah Mahaffy, to report what I pictured does not do the same job as saying which Sarah I meant. If you ask 'whom did you mean?' and I reply that I pictured so and so, you can still ask whether that was whom I meant. I might have pictured her because the Sarah I meant always reminds me of this other Sarah, or to illustrate to myself whom I did not mean. Or the picturing might have occurred for no reason that I can think of.

Similarly, if I make a threat, I may grit my teeth and have feelings of grim determination, but if in making the threat I also tell the person threatened about this, that will not do the job of telling him I mean the threat. 'Did you mean it?' 'I gritted my teeth and felt grim.' To this one could reply 'Touching; but you have not told me whether you meant it.'

We tend to fasten on cases in which there is something happening like picturing something, gritting teeth, or having grim feelings, because the surface grammar leads us to expect that meaning is *something,* and it is not easy to think what else it might be; but in most cases of the kind we are here considering in which the word 'mean' is aptly used there is just nothing that is even faintly plausible to serve as the action, process or event of meaning. 'When you said yesterday that Peter had a good sense of humour, did you mean that man over there in the red shirt?' 'Yes, he's the one.' 'But you didn't know then that he would be here and wearing a red shirt.' 'When you said you were going to Montreal tomorrow, did you mean it?' 'Yes.' 'And what form did your meaning it take?' 'It didn't take any form. I just said it. In saying now that I meant it I only mean that my saying it was a normal case of saying something. Nothing tricky going on.' (Cf. *PI* §§187, 692–3; *BB* 39.)

Then how *is* this word used, if not to record something that went on alongside of one's saying something? It is used quite variously (an 'odd job' word), but a consideration of two rather different cases may provide characteristic models, starting from which others may be constructed as variations.

Meaning it. In the case of threats, offers, surprising assertions, or anything about which another person may want to be quite sure, we may be asked if we meant it; or we may without being asked volunteer that we meant it, to drive a point home.

It is characteristic of these cases that there had better not be any serious unclarity or ambiguity in what one says. This is because 'I meant it' means 'What I said may be taken at its face value.' If what I said has no face value, it will be senseless to direct taking it at that value.

If I say it is five o'clock on the sun, there either can't be a question whether I mean it, or at least there is a prior question what I meant.

It is plausible to compare saying 'I meant it' to crossing one's heart when saying something, a further action we can perform that perhaps was once supposed to bring down the divine wrath if we are lying. Similarly there is a convention that if a person, having said something, adds that she means it, she will lose credibility if she fails to stand by her offer, carry out her threat, act as she would if she believed her assertion, and so on. By adding that we mean it, we preclude ourselves from later backing off, saying that we were only joking, or that we were emotionally wrought up and didn't realize what we were saying; and by taking this step we run risks of embarrassment that would not be so great had we not added that we meant it.

That is the way this game is played. Knowing that someone has courted the social risks involved in adding that she means her threat, we are apt to take it more seriously. Our reason for taking it seriously is not that we believe her when she says meaning it is going on, and we know from experience that when *that* is happening, we had better watch out!

This step not only involves risks, but may have advantages. Another person, knowing the risks we are running, will be more likely to take what we said seriously, just as he might if he saw a believer incurring the divine wrath by crossing his heart.

The question whether to say we mean it is one, not of whether something called meaning it is going on, but of whether to run the risks incurred by so speaking. If we wondered whether to say we meant it, it would be prospective, not introspective, thinking we would need to do.

'Do you mean it?' is like 'Will you say that again, given that if you repeat it now, you'll be held to it?', and 'I said it and I meant it' is like 'I said it and I say it again with the understanding that now I may be held to it.' We say it again, but under new and more restrictive auspices, which auspices we ourselves invoke in saying we mean it. That is the kind of instrument this is.

An objection: won't it be safe to run these risks if we do mean it, just as it is safe to tell someone your pockets are empty if they are empty? In the latter case there is some risk of embarrassment if it turns out that the pockets are not empty, but no amount of thinking about this risk will be so useful in deciding whether to say there is something in one's pockets as an examination of the pockets themselves. Similarly will not the self-awareness that shows whether we mean it be the decisive consideration?

This might be a telling objection if we knew what meaning it was, in the kind of way we know what having coins in our pockets is, and hence could investigate whether it prevailed. But there is nothing we call meaning it, and when we make a threat and add that we mean it, we are not recording the occurrence of the phenomenon of meaning it, but making the threat more emphatic. It is sound if unhelpful advice to say 'Don't say you mean it unless you do mean it', but it is nonsense to say 'Don't say you mean it unless meaning it is occurring.' It is not as if we all knew that, when meaning the threat one has made is occurring, it is much more likely that the threat will be carried out. The connection here is not between a phenomenon and the effects of its having occurred, but rather between the performance of a significant speech act and the entitlement that this act confers.

A different objection: suppose I threaten that I will do *this* unless you do *that*. You in fact act as demanded, and so there is no occasion for me to carry out the threat. Later you ask 'Did you mean it?' and I say I did. I can't in this case be putting myself in a position where it will be more embarrassing to me if I do not carry out my threat, because there is no longer a question of my doing this. What is the function of 'I meant it' in this event?

I find it difficult to be sure how to handle this objection, but it is at least clear that the question 'Did you mean it?' cannot be answered 'No, I forgot to', or 'I don't know. I didn't notice whether I did or not', or 'Yes, I remember distinctly meaning it.' The question whether I meant it is not about whether something called meaning it was done, or happened.

It is clear too that the question 'Did you mean it?' is tantamount to 'Would you actually have carried out the threat?', and the reply 'Yes, I did' is tantamount to 'Yes, I would have.' But it is difficult to be clear what kind of speech act this is. I am inclined to suggest the following: when we say we mean a threat, an offer, or what have you, it shows something about us – in different cases, that we care about the issue giving rise to the threat, or that we are ruthless, or generous. It does not show that the phenomenon of meaning them occurred. After-the-event professions to have meant it perform the act of identifying oneself with what, in a given case, having meant it would show. This may be a *defiant* act, if it is ruthlessness that is shown. One is displaying, not reporting, ruthlessness – witness the fact that one might say 'You're damn right I did.' 'I meant it' is not like 'I have done many ruthless things.' The latter is a confession of ruthlessness, the former a show of it.

Meaning this rather than that. Examples of this are saying something about Peter, meaning this Peter rather than that, saying something ambiguous and later disambiguating it, and so on. This kind of use of 'mean' requires a different analysis. Saying what one means or meant is obviously not repeating what one said but under more restrictive circumstances, nor could we say that it is a linguistic convention that saying 'I meant such and such' commits one more fully to what one has said. Until what one said is clarified, there is not yet anything to which one might commit oneself. ('I don't know what I mean by this, but I do mean it' is a grammatical joke.)

It should not be necessary to show at any length that we are not recording something we did or experienced at the time at which we say we meant such and such. I say something about Martha's ketch. You say 'By a ketch, did you mean a sailboat with its mizzen mast forward of the rudder post, or aft of it?'. I reply that I meant the former. I will not usually have asked myself, before referring to Martha's ketch, whether it is a ketch or a yawl, or reviewed what I know about how to tell the difference. I know day in, day out that her boat is a ketch, and I have a similarly unepisodic knowledge of what a ketch is. In enormous numbers of cases we just routinely say something. Nothing of any interest or relevance happens as we say it, whether in the mind or elsewhere. If, later, a question what we meant arises, it may as in the above example, be answered with the greatest of ease; but for this we draw, not on what happened at the time of speaking, but on such resources as the fact that we can say any old time what a ketch is. In saying 'I meant the kind with the mizzen mast forward of the rudder post', we do seem to be saying what happened, but there is nothing that happens that we call meaning this, and so we must look elsewhere for an account of how this word is used.

I would propose what might be called a directive theory. 'What (or whom) did you mean?' can be translated 'How should I take that?', and 'I meant thus and so' can be translated 'Take what I said thusly' or 'I direct that you take it thusly.'

The appearance of reporting something one did or under-went is eliminated by these translations. 'Take it thusly' does not even appear to make a representation about oneself at the time of speaking, and 'How should I take it?' does not even seem to inquire about the speaker. 'I direct. . .' may appear to say something about oneself, but at least not about oneself at the time of speaking; and anyway one thing that is very clear about performatives is that they do not report anything. Saying those words *is* directing.

There is a difficulty here, however, 'Take it this way' does not seem to include the assurance that 'I meant it in such and such a way seems to include, an assurance that the present directive does not involve a change of attitude. To restore this assurance, the words 'Take it this way. This is the way it was meant' come naturally to hand; but of course we must not say that, because it is sentences like 'that is the way it was meant' that we are trying to understand.

The difficulty here lies in the fact that in posing it we are mixing the language to be translated and the language that translates it. 'Take it this way. This is how it was meant' seems to be a way of expressing the assurance that was felt to be lacking given just the first of these sentences, but when we remember that in the second sentence we are at least in part directing how it should be taken, it becomes very much less clear whether the conjunction of the two sentences makes for redundancy – whether it does not come down to 'Take it this way. This is the way to take it.' If there were a language like English, but lacking this use of 'to mean', in which instead of that verb people always used explicit directives, we could not *in that language* say 'The English "I meant thus and so" means "Take it this way. This is the way it was meant."' In giving translations for philosophical purposes we are in effect constructing English-like languages, lacking the words or expressions we are translating.

If this shows that we cannot express the difficulty antiseptically by saying that we need to add 'That is how it was meant' (or any such synonymous constructions as 'That is how it was intended'), it does not show that there is not a difficulty, or that the proposed translation is adequate. What we need is a translation that captures the assurance expressed in 'That is how it was meant', but without using the problem word.

For this I would suggest saying that 'I meant thus and so' means 'Take it thusly, and in saying this I am saying again what I said before, only more clearly', or 'I assure you that the following is a re-statement of what I said earlier, which should not be so ambiguous. . .' Here we get away from the picture of having meant thus and so as something else that went on at the time.

When we say something, if another person does not understand, we can try again but, neither when we first spoke, nor when we try again, is there something mysterious called 'what we mean' that we are trying to cast into words, and that we may be more or less successful in capturing. It may seem very puzzling how it is that we can try again, and how we know whether we have succeeded in 'saying what we meant', if there is nothing called 'what we mean' that we may capture in words or fail to capture, but it is at least clear that there is no such thing, and it is only a misunderstanding of expressions like 'what I meant' that leads us to suppose otherwise.

The question how we arrive at explanations of what we mean might in part be answered in terms of our general comprehension of language. Given some linguistic skill, we can take a sentence we have not ourselves asserted, see how it might mean various things, and construct sentences that bring out and contrast these various meanings. For example a sentence like 'George IV wanted to know if Scott wrote *Waverly* may report any one of the following: (a) the king asked 'Did Scott write *Waverly;* (b) the king, pointing to a book, asked 'Did Scott write that book?', or (c) pointing to a man who was in fact Scott, the king asked 'Did that man write *Waverly*?', or (d) pointing to the same man and to a book that was in fact *Waverly*, the king asked 'Did that man write that book?'. When, having said something and been misunderstood, we explain what we meant, we are at least in part using this skill,

33

which can operate independently of our current conversational aims or problems.

Of the sentences that might in the abstract elucidate senses of what we said, how do we know which one explains what we meant? By whether we are content to have another person go away with it as our opinion, our offer, our report. When someone says 'Did you mean this or this?', we decide by thinking about the sentences proffered, asking ourselves 'Can I endorse this?' 'Did you mean such and such?' is an invitation to subscribe to such and such, and we might decide by thinking about whether it was true, or about whether it would suit our purposes to have this person believe we subscribe to it.

I have been suggesting that the question what kind of instrument 'to mean' is can be answered, at least for the two uses discussed, by saying it is a quasi-performative. That is how it works. It is not a standard performative, since we do not say 'I hereby mean . . .' and we do not mean something *by* saying we mean it (or by doing anything else); but we are taking a characteristic performative plunge in saying 'I mean it'; and we can translate 'I meant thus and so' using performative words such as 'I direct. . .'.

There is again not much evidence bearing on whether Wittgenstein would agree with any of this, except what I have said about what meaning is *not*. Most of what he says, for example in *PI* §§661-93, is negative in that way; but consider *PI* §557:

> Now, when I uttered the double negation, what constituted my meaning it as a strengthened negative and not as an affirmative? There is no answer running: 'It consisted in the fact that. . .' In certain circumstances instead of saying 'This duplication is meant as a strengthening', I can pronounce it as a strengthening.

He does not enlarge on this, but the *pronouncing* that he speaks of here is clearly a performative act.

In *PI* §334 we read

> 'So you really wanted to say. . .' – We use this phrase in order to lead someone from one form of expression to another.

'You wanted to say' and 'You meant' are used interchangeably in such contexts, and hence Wittgenstein might likewise have said that 'I meant. . .' is used to lead someone from one form of expression to another; and since the same could be said of 'Take it this way. . .', Wittgenstein here comes quite close to my directive account of some uses of 'to mean'.

Again, in *PI* §692 there is an echo of my suggestion that one's explanation of what one meant by a ketch derives from one's ability to say any old time what a ketch is. Wittgenstein says:

> Is it correct for someone to say: 'When I gave you this rule, I meant you to. . . in this case'? Even [sic] if he did not think of this case at all when he gave the rule? Of course it is correct. For 'to mean it' did not mean: to think of it. But now the problem is: how are we to judge whether someone meant such and such? – the fact that he has, for example, mastered a particular technique in arithmetic and algebra, and that he taught someone else the expansion of a series in the usual way, is such a criterion.

Wittgenstein adverts here to mastery of a technique. My example was different, but in both cases an acquired, day in, day out ability is being exercised when one says what one meant.

One might take the point a step beyond where Wittgenstein takes it, and suggest that to say 'I meant you to. . . in the case' is to *pronounce* or *declare* something to be the correct step to take, and similarly to say 'By a ketch I meant. . .' is to assert or declare that to be what a ketch is.

1.2.5 Love

The word 'love' is used in at least two rather different cases: – when we speak of our love for children, grandparents, friends or God; and when we declare our love for another person, as in 'I am in love with you'. In the latter kind of case we may equally say 'I love you', but we do not talk indifferently of loving or being in love with children, grandparents, good friends or God, although it may be possible, if rare and worrisome, for people to be in love in the latter cases.

We do not often worry much about whether we exactly love a child, because it will not make much difference whether we love or merely are greatly interested in and enjoy it; but whether one is in love is a question of greater consequence, that may exercise the putative lover, the putative beloved, or other people, and is of some difficulty.

In dealing with this question it might appear desirable to

know what love is. With that information in hand one could check oneself over to see how far one's thoughts, feelings or behaviour constituted an authentic case of being in love. Here it might not be necessary that there be only one set of criteria. There might be half a dozen or an indefinite number of them but, however many there were, it would still be necessary that each of the sets constitute a workable decision procedure, for example tell us that if you are *A* and *B* and *C* and not *D*, you are in love.

How might it be settled whether any suggested set of criteria would if satisfied show a person to be in love?

At a time when marriages were indissoluble and the expression 'in love' was used most notably in proposing marriage, the question might have arisen, how can we tell whether our present feeling for another person is such as to guarantee, or even make it quite likely, that a life-long union will be happy or rewarding? It might have been found, or might have been promulgated by people claiming to know, that all and only people in such and such states had successful marriages, and we might thus have come to call any of those states 'being in love'.

Any particular findings or reputed findings might of course turn out to be gravely in error, but at least the method, of working out which states provided some assurance of a happy life-long union, is a conceivable way of settling what love is: and, if we take that question to be answerable at all, it is difficult to think of any other kind of method that would enable us to settle it in a workmanlike manner. If we went around studying and interviewing people who said they were in love, that method would presuppose that they were indeed in love, which would be just the question our findings were intended to settle.

Yet if the first-described method is a workable way of settling *something*, it is not clear that it would show what *love* is. We would need in addition a way of deciding whether love is whatever present state of a person provides some assurance of a happy life-long union. That assumption might have been plausible when marriage was the only condition under which a man and woman could reputably live together, and when declaring love was tantamount to proposing marriage, but when (as now) a declaration of love leaves open the question of whether marriage is being proposed, the assumption loses the plausibility it derived from the erstwhile close connection between love and marriage.

Moreover it is in any event extremely unlikely that there should be a present condition of a person that would provide significant assurance that a life-long union would not be regretted; and it has never been seriously contended that there are such states. Some people may believe that there are, as an inference from the fact that one of the times we say we are in love is in the course of proposing marriage; and these people may, if they propose marriage themselves, believe that the state they are in provides some assurance that the union proposed will not be regretted; but no one claims to know which states provide that assurance, or to know, rather than suppose, that they are themselves in such a state.

Hence it is antecedently unlikely that there is an answer to the question what love, conceived as a state, is. That is not to say that the answer has yet to be discovered, but that the question contains a mistake, the mistake of supposing that the word 'love' is used to record the existence of a characteristic state, (or one of a set of such states), or that it is used to express the belief or the hunch that the state one is in will one day be found to have been love.

If a man declares his love for a woman, she may indeed suspect that he is a philanderer and is not in love, but more than one understanding of this suspicion is possible. If, in line with what has just been argued, she is not suspecting him of saying falsely such things as that he delights in her presence, is disconsolate in her absence, is jealous of her other male friends, or any other set of feelings or patterns of behaviour, – her suspicion might still be thought of in a quite different way. She might be suspecting that whereas he purported to be offering to enter a certain kind of pair-bonding relationship with her, he had no intention of standing by that offer.

It is mostly people who 'delight in her presence, are disconsolate in her absence' and so on, who make such offers, but a philanderer might be every bit as enthusiastic about the person for whom he declares love as a person whose declaration can be taken seriously; and if the declaration is an offer, it does not record such enthusiasm, but sets out, albeit implicitly, what is being offered.

It is true that suspecting the absence of this enthusiasm is a reason for being suspicious of the offer, but still the latter of these suspicions is distinct from the former.

If suspecting he is a philanderer is suspecting he has no intention to stand by his offer, we could still not say what is present in the normal case and missing in the philanderer. If an undevious person makes an offer, there is nothing alongside of his making it that is his intention to stand by it if it is accepted. He just says 'I offer thus and so', and will of course stand by it. His offer is not a report of his intention. Apart from the fact that he is not a devious person (which is not something he is currently experiencing) there is nothing to report. We shall need some elaboration of what kind of pair-bonding is offered or proposed, but that a declaration of love is some kind of offer or proposal is confirmed by the fact that if Mary says 'John, do you love me?', and he replies 'Well, I think of you night and day, I'm drunk with pleasure when I am with you and I yearn for you terribly when I'm not. I have lost interest in other women and it makes me frantic when I see other men flirting with you...', what he says is typical enough of people in love, but the significant thing is that he should hang back from saying 'Yes, I do.' He is talking as if he didn't know whether he loved her, and was trying to work it out by reviewing the evidence. He is like a jeweller who, when asked if he guarantees this watch, goes on and on about its excellent materials and workmanship. The customer might be glad enough to hear all this, but it stops short of answering the question 'Do you or do you not guarantee it?'. Similarly what a beloved wants to hear is an actual declaration of love. No matter how long one has gone on recording joy, enthusiasm, tenderness, jealousy and so on, a new plunge is taken in saying 'I am in love with you.'

There is a popular saying that, if you are in love, you will know it. This may suggest that either there is something peculiarly striking that people feel as well as joy, tenderness and so on, which leaves them in no doubt, or that the joy and tenderness sometimes have a distinctive quality, the experience of which removes doubt; but, if there is wisdom in this saying, it may rather be an oblique way of making the point that if an undevious person can not right away take the step of declaring love, if he reviews the evidence, that itself shows that he is not in love. There is doubt here, but it is not about whether one's present feelings constitute love, but rather about whether to utter the significant words 'I love you'. And this reluctance, this hanging back from taking the plunge, not the particular set of feelings that have been described, will be the significant thing.

So far I have been arguing that a declaration of love is not a report but a significant speech act, and I have not addressed myself to the question what its significance is. Largely because of changes in the moral climate that have occurred in the past quarter century, the latter is now a somewhat unsettled question, and it may be that for many scrupulous people all that is clear is that a declaration of love is somehow a momentous step, not to be entered on lightly. One knows that different people may expect different things given such a declaration, but anyone who was not just casual about the use of the word 'love' would suppose that *some* kind of deepening of the relationship was hoped for, even if nothing could be taken as understood regarding what form that deepening might take. Even this minimal attitude would be enough to sustain my contention that saying one is in love is a significant speech act.

However it would be clearer how these affairs work if we set before ourselves in some detail a possible account of the significance of a declaration of love. To avoid any suggestion that this is a correct account, I will cast it as the story of an imaginary institution. Suppose that long ago, before Christianity or anything much like it emerged, there was a social reformer who conceived the idea of a relationship that could be fashioned between a man and a woman in which two persons became as one for the begetting and raising of children, the arranging of food and shelter, the conduct of friendships and the pursuit of pleasures. His idea was that, when people were paired in this way, each of them would come to regard the interests of the unit they comprised as their own interest. They would make decisions about all matters of importance jointly, and neither of them would begrudge time or effort expended in the common interest. Although they would often initially have divergent preferences, when they had reached an agreement in such a case, what they agreed upon would become the preference of each of them; and they would say 'we prefer', 'we want', 'we intend', etc. as routinely as other people use the first person singular construction with such verbs.

Suppose that our visionary went about describing and

praising this kind of relationship, and many people were attracted, and interested in trying it. Because it was somewhat complex, a short way of proposing it seemed desirable, so it was suggested that, instead of detailing the kind of relationship contemplated, a person proposing it should just say 'I am in love with you', and it would be conventionally understood what this meant. Let's suppose that nothing was laid down regarding the duration of such a bond. It was recognized on all sides that it would be somewhat difficult to fashion and sustain, and all that was expected of people embarking on it was that they should not lightly abandon the effort.

We can see in his example that something a bit complex is proposed, and that whether anyone wished to participate in an arrangement such as this would be a question whether, having examined and thought about the details of it, they found they could opt for it. Whether someone wished to embark on it with a particular person would be a question of how believable it was that, with that person, the arrangement would prove livable. In either case it would be a *prospective* question. People would dwell on the specifications of the type of relationship they would be undertaking, and on the question how well it promised to work out in the particular case of themselves and *this* person.

We are of course imagining a somewhat unreal state of affairs in which the issues are much clearer than they are in the present social atmosphere. Anyone is likely to feel that affairs of the heart are not as ponderable as they might be in the imagined state of affairs. But there is a pattern discernible in the example, that may still remain if, for the relatively clear features of the picture, we substitute uncertainty and confusion about what a declaration of love proposes, or even about whether it proposes anything. What remains is the thought, which would be widely accepted, that a declaration of love is in some way, however unclear, momentous.

To return to the confusion in which we find ourselves about the significance of a declaration of love, this will greatly reduce the ponderability of affairs of the heart, and perhaps explain why they are so called, but will not take away the fact that a declaration of love is a move towards the establishment (or the preservation) of some kind of relationship, or the fact that among scrupulous users of the word it will be a serious and special relationship. Thus we see people greatly excited by one another hanging back from saying they are in love, although they could not at all explain under what conditions they would have no qualms about saying it; and when they do come to be able to say it, it may still not be clear to them what new element this introduces; but it will be clear that something important has been said. Questions may now arise that might previously have seemed fanciful, such as 'Do you want to take up with me to the exclusion of others?' or 'Are you suggesting a long-term relationship between us?' In asking any such question it need not be assumed that this is one of the things a declaration of love certainly entails, but being a possible new development of some moment, and being one of the consequences of declaring love in times past, it is a question that may now fairly be raised.

'Love' on this reading is not a performative word. We do not say 'I hereby love you', and saying one loves is not loving, the way saying one promises is promising; but a declaration of love is *like* a performative in being a significant speech act, a further plunge that, after describing one's feelings, one may hesitate to take. It gets us into something we do not get into merely by describing feelings. The significance of a declaration of love is at present unclear, but it is at least fairly clear that declaring love is a step of some moment, taking us well beyond, for example 'I think you're delightful'. And while there are no certainties concerning what we are getting into, neither is there an absolute void. There are some things that clearly may be in the offing, among them being marriage, or in the present moral climate a marriage-like relationship which neither is publicly solemnized nor includes any undertaking regarding its duration, but is still a two-becoming-as-one relationship.

It may well be thought that however interesting this may be as a theory, it is simply too sophisticated. Isn't love obviously a state we may be in? Don't we see it in the fondness of the gaze, the eagerness of the response, the ease and confidence with which lovers interact, their general euphoria? Might it not be better to say that, when people are in that state, they find it natural to go on to some form of pair-bonding, but that saying they are in love only records the state they are in, and that what they may therefore do is something further? Don't people say 'I am in love with you. Will you marry me?', and doesn't this show that proposals, whether of marriage or any other kind of bonding, are distinct from, if closely connected with, declarations of love?

The question whether love is a discernible state is not settled by the fact that it is often obvious that a person is in love. What we see may be an offshoot of what has been happening. Peter and Emily have been seeing a lot of one another and they get on unusually well together.They both have known other people they have found comparably attractive, but it has not often happened that the attraction has been mutual. So they are elated. Their eyes sparkle. They feel buoyant and eager for life. Here clearly it is the fact that their relationship is developing so splendidly that is the primary thing, and this lifts their spirits. If one of them said 'I am in love with you', just to be saying this might heighten the elation. The elation would then be an effect of being able to say this, and saying it would not be saying one was elated.

It may be that there is a characteristic kind of elation that comes from being in love, and we can see that someone is in love when we see this kind of elation, but still there is a distinction between the elation and its cause.

Does 'I am in love and I want to marry you' say two different things? I certainly appears so, but that might be because, as I have suggested, 'I am in love' is an oblique form of expression. We might say that 'I am in love and want to marry you', is about the same as saying 'I am in love with you *that is to say* I want to marry you'. People might express themselves this way in recognition of the fact that not everyone will be sure what 'I am in love with you', means, and that there is a need to remove this uncertainty.

The 'but' in 'I am in love with you but I shan't propose' brings out the fact that the first part of that sentence generates an expectation that has to be cancelled by the second part. [In saying flatly that this expectation is generated I am ignoring the complications discussed above (p. 40-1), arising from the confusion into which we have drifted about the significance of declarations of love.]

If the above is a plausible account of at least the scrupulous use of the word 'love', showing it to be a kind of quasi-performative, still no evidence has been adduced that it is an account to which Wittgenstein might subscribe. There is not much evidence on this, but in *Z* 504 we read:

Love is not a feeling. Love is put to the test, pain not. One does not say: 'That is not true pain, or it would not have gone off so quickly.'

The implied suggestion is that we do say the corresponding thing about love. That seems right enough. If one day it is Jill that Jack is excited about and the next day it is Jennifer, we would not say it was love, no matter what it felt like. But this might only show that love has to be a feeling of some duration. Or it might show that love is like grief, which Wittgenstein compared to pain in a similar way. (*PI* p. 174). There he said of the word 'grief' that it describes a pattern in the weave of our lives; and this probably means that it is not just a feeling that lasts for a time, or that occurs on certain sorts of occasion, but that, if it includes feelings, still it may also include other things, perhaps thoughts and actions.

This would still be quite different from what I have been contending about love. If love too were a pattern in the weave of our lives, we would check for it by seeing whether the characteristic pattern (or if there were many such, one of them) prevailed. John could answer Mary's question whether he loved her by reporting enough about his recent thoughts, feelings and actions. There would be no speech act that he might, significantly, find hard to perform, just as there is none in the case of grieving.

However, it may be that Wittgenstein chose an unfortunate example of 'putting to the test', in the question of duration. If we made a distinction between testing in the sense of checking, and putting to the test, where the former involves looking more carefully or looking further afield, matching what one finds to a set of criteria, and the latter involves doing something calculated to beget a reaction, to which reaction significance is attached, then Z 504 might come out more clearly as providing textual support.

The following might be one model of 'putting to the test'. I tell a typewriter salesman I want this machine and I'll be back for it tomorrow. He has been told this before and the customer has not returned, so he asks for a deposit. If I am unwilling to leave a deposit he does not count on my returning. I have made an undertaking and he puts it to the test by seeing whether I will back up my words with deeds. Why does he count on my returning if I make a deposit? Not because he then knows something about the state I am in, but because it will now be disadvantageous to me not to complete the purchase.

Clearly if (though perhaps not only if) a declaration of love were like making an undertaking, it might be put to the test in comparable ways. Or things might have happened that would constitute a putting to the test, even if they did not occur as a result of anyone's intention to run a test. 'What would I do for the person I say I love?' Or 'What have I done that constitutes passing a test of my love?' 'If I buy her a gift, do I do it in the hope of winning her favour, or because her interests have become mine?' 'If she needed medical treatments that would cost a great deal of money, would I begrudge my share of this expense?' 'If she wished to study architecture and I would have to support her while she did, would I be in favour of this only if it seemed likely to make us richer in the long run?' And so on.

In *PI* §587 Wittgenstein says:

> It makes sense to ask, 'Do I really love her, or am I only pretending to myself? and the process of introspection is the calling up of memories; of imagined possible situations, and of the feelings I would have if. . .

That process is not what philosophers usually think of as introspection, although it is among the things a person ordinarily called introspective does; but clearly it is a process of 'putting oneself to the test': not of checking oneself over to see whether what is there conforms to a model, but of generating reactions by putting testing questions to oneself, and of reviewing past reactions to testing situations.

Wittgenstein did not say what kind of 'imagined possible situations' he had in mind, or what feelings he reckoned it would be significant that one should have in those situations, but the situations and feelings I just described would be obvious candidates. And the reason one might consider *these* situations and *these* feelings is derived from a conception of what one is proposing in declaring love, namely a relationship in which two become one.

The significance of declarations of love being in a state of some confusion, other people might have different conceptions and hence put different questions to themselves, but the pattern in which what is proposed generates the questions would be the same. Hence these passages are at least reconcilable with the picture I have suggested. They clearly support the negative part of my view, even if they include no distinct suggestion that 'love', in the uses discussed here, is a quasi-performative word.

2.2.6 Explanations of attitudes

In the four parts of this subsection I will discuss various ways in which we *enlarge* on what our attitude is. Later (in Section 2.3) I will draw attention to some ways in which what we say, without declaring an attitude, still *shows* an attitude, and would be inept if one's attitude were otherwise.

Whereas so far it has been individual words I have been trying to display as being in some sense instruments, in this section I shall be dealing with a variety of utterances that mostly do not call for the use of any particular word or expression. 'I should have liked to stay longer'. 'I am leaving, but not because you told me to', and 'With some encouragement from you, I might very well do it' are some examples.

The first of the above sentences is a standard civility often to be heard as guests leave parties, but the third is likely to have been put together *ad hoc* as a way of explaining an attitude towards a step of some consequence that someone has perhaps said she is tempted to take. It is something she might say in response to the question how serious she is about the contemplated step; and one of the things she might alternatively have said is 'I suppose it is just a daydream really, but it is one to which I am greatly attached.'

The fact that indefinite numbers of these explanations of attitude may be constructed makes them difficult to discuss in a general way, but the treatment of a few of them may provide some models, given which one can shift for oneself in other cases.

'I should have liked to stay longer'. Does this mean 'If I were to stay longer, I would enjoy it'? If in saying this we are calculating what would happen if. . ., we might express ourselves in ways that brought out the coldness of the calculation: 'It is virtually certain that if I were to stay I would enjoy it', 'All the indications are that if. . .', and so on. But these latter ways of speaking would not come across as expressions of regret. From them another person might conclude that one is probably regretting having to leave, but one has stopped short of actually saying this.

If a person is leaving reluctantly, it may be, but needn't be, because she reckons there would be more pleasure to come if she stayed. She may have other reasons. Perhaps it is obvious that the hostess would be pleased if she were to stay, and she would have liked to oblige. Or perhaps she fears that other people, seeing someone leave, will also be moved to depart. But she is not, in saying she would have liked to stay longer, saying which of these or other reasons she has.

One can reckon there would be more pleasure to come if one stayed, without regretting leaving, for example if one is not gravely addicted to pleasure, or if one is going on to an even better party.

'I should have liked to stay longer' does not give a reason for regretting leaving, but is another way of saying one regrets this. But how does 'I regret having to leave' work? Does it report how one feels, or is saying it like sighing or looking distressed? Does it mean 'I am inclined to sigh', or is it the articulate form of a sigh?

Suppose I decided half an hour ago that I would have to leave soon, and have been feeling sad ever since. Would 'I regret having to leave' be a way of saying that I have been moping for the past half hour? One could sincerely express regrets even if one had not been moping, but had gone on enjoying the party; and if one only began feeling sad when one finally got up to leave, it would not follow that before that point one had not regretted having to leave.

One might be quite cheerful in taking one's leave, for example if the hosts are dear friends and one is happy, even while leaving, to be there and talking to them. This may be part of the reason one regrets leaving. In that case one cannot say one is sad, or even that he will be sad. One may go away reflecting contentedly on the visit or the party.

Expressions of regret are best said in regretful tones and accompanied by wistful smiles or regretful gestures. That is what one would expect if they were doing the same duty as the smiles or gestures. It might be clear enough from one's countenance that one regretted leaving but, even so, saying that one regretted it would, among friends, remove any uncertainty.

Saying one regrets is a form regret may take. It is a verbal display of regret. Putting it that way may suggest that there is something called regret that exists independently of its expression in words or gestures or wistful smiles. But talking about displays or expressions of regret may be confusing in a way like that in which saying 'These two sentences express the same proposition' can confuse us. We might be led by the

latter assertion to wonder what kind of phenomena propositions are, and in what kind of relation they stand to the
sentences that express them, but all we mean is that the two
sentences can be used interchangeably. Similarly we need
only be saying about regret that there are various more or less
equivalent forms of it, some of them verbal.

When I say that wistful smiles or regretful gestures may do
the same duty as saying one regrets, what is this 'duty'? There
is an expression 'to give someone one's regrets'. It can be one's
saying one regrets having to leave that people are glad of. In
the normal case one says this and means it too, even if some
people say it disingenuously and to be polite. We are apt to
think that the difference between the sincere and the disin-
genuous case is that a feeling lies behind the former and is
pretended in the latter, and that revealing this feeling is the job
the words properly do. What I am suggesting by contrast is that
'I regret having to leave', like 'I thank you' or 'I apologize', is
an utterance the saying of which is itself significant. It is the
fact that I have said it that another person may be glad of. If
there were a custom in which, to establish friendship, we
shook both another person's hands with arms crossed, people
might be glad one made this gesture, in a way like the way they
might be glad of one's expression of regret.

'But not because you told me to'. These words may sound
as if they were denying the current existence of a causal
connection that one supposes would exist in the case in which
one did something obediently. The picture is like this: there
are two cases, in both of which I hear myself being ordered to
leave, and I do leave. In the case in which I leave obediently,
a connection can be traced between the hearing and the
leaving. What I hear may lead me to have the thought 'He'll be
furious if I don't go'; this may cause me to feel fear; and the fear
may cause me to leave. In the other case there is also a causal
chain leading to my leaving, but it is traceable back, not to my
hearing the order, but to my feeling thirsty, remembering a
dentist appointment, or what have you. Since an observer can
only see the input and the output, and they are the same in
both cases, I need to tell him whether the two were connected,
and when I say 'but not because you told me to', I report that
they were not.

Yet if on hearing the order I say to myself 'I'll not leave just
because *he* tells me!', that is a thought that would represent a

break in the supposed causal chain in just the way feeling thirsty or remembering a dentist appointment might, but this thought is not an observation on the process leading to whatever I do, but a *part* of it. Clearly however the word 'because' is used here in just the way it is used in'. . . but not because you told me to', and if it is not a causal 'because' in the former case, it is not one in the latter case either.

If my being ordered to leave reminded me that I had a dentist appointment, whereupon I of course left, then if these connections are causal at all, there would be an unbroken causal chain between hearing the order and leaving, but it would not be a case in which I left because I was told to.

If I was attending a seminar on Wittgenstein and the subject of toothache came up, reminding me of a dentist appointment, and I left, I would say I left because I remembered a dentist appointment, not because someone had asked how we know where the pain is, although the latter can be regarded as a cause of my going if my hearing an order can. If I did say I left because someone asked that question, I would at least most naturally be taken to be declaring myself opposed to or bored by that kind of discussion, rather than to be tracing a causal chain.

In making points like this one need not deny that there is a causal explanation of whatever a person does. That is not the issue. It is whether in saying 'I did it because. . .', we are talking about the cause in a particular case. The objection to that supposition is not that what we say in such cases is a crude or unscientific causal representation, but that it is not of that type at all.

If one thinks 'I'm not going to leave just because he tells me', that is a defiant thought, and similarly to say 'I'm leaving, but not because you told me' is a defiant act. By saying this one *takes the step* of defying the person who issued the order. This *may* be all bluster and bravado. In many cases in which a person does leave, purporting to have some other reason for doing so, she would perhaps not dream of remaining; but even so it is defiant of her to speak this way.

Bluster or not, it may be that it is her being an independent sort of person (or her wanting to think of herself that way), that makes her say this, but even so she is not *saying* she is an independent sort. If she has a history of this kind of defiance, the present speech act is not a report of that history, but another item in it.

If we take the case in which someone obediently leaves when ordered to do so, and later says 'I left because so and so told me', his speech act is no longer defiant, but still does not record a causal link between his being ordered and his leaving. He is not saying anything like 'Once the order was given, I just couldn't help myself leaving. It was as if I were under the control of an invisible agent', but rather announcing where he stands on such matters. It is like saying 'It is my policy to obey so and so's orders.'

If in yet another case he answered the question why he left by saying 'I don't recognize his authority, but I left because I thought it unwise to create a scene by remaining', he would be making two policy declarations. The second part of what he said may seem to say that a thought occurred, causing him to leave; but for him to express himself as he did there need have been no moment when he was having that thought, as we can see from the fact that he might equally have said'. . . because I *think* it unwise in such cases to create a scene'. He might be saying 'this is the way I handle such matters', and indicating how he justifies that policy. But, even if the thought that it would be unwise to create a scene did run through his head, his subsequent speech act does not just record that occurrence, but *endorses* the thought he therein had. And he would not be saying that, once the thought made its appearance, his departure was involuntary, but that, to leave being the course of action indicated by the thought, he left.

Policy declarations are fairly clearly quasi-performatives. In them one commits oneself *pro tem* to act as the policy directs in comparable cases.

Wittgenstein raised this issue in *PI* §487ff., and when he said 'Does this proposition ["I am leaving the room because you tell me to"] *describe* a connexion between my action and his order; or does it make the connexion?', there is little doubt that his answer would be 'the latter'. However he does not enlarge on the sense in which the connection is made. What I have suggested might be one way in which this thought could be developed.

How serious one is. 'I have been toying with the idea of writing a novel.' 'How serious are you about this? Isn't it just a pipe dream?' How does one answer questions like this?

If there were something called seriousness, a feeling perhaps in which thoughts were bathed, and if the feeling could be more or less intense, we might locate a current feeling roughly on a scale of intensity, and thus indicate how serious we were. But no one says 'My feeling is quite like it has been on past occasions when I have gone on to do the thing I had been contemplating doing, so I think I can say I am quite serious.' If there is a feeling in which thoughts are bathed, it can be much the same whether we are having a pipe dream or seriously considering something.

We can generally say how serious we are. As a way of finding out what we mean by this, we might focus on cases in which the fact that we went ahead with a plan showed that we had been serious, to see what we could notice about ourselves that might be our seriousness. But this method would imply that before we conducted this inquiry we did not know what seriousness was, and ought not to have been able to use the word.

We do say 'I feel fairly serious about it', and that may suggest that seriousness is a feeling, but in fact the word 'feel' is used here in much the way it is used in 'I feel it would be a mistake'. There it is used in preference to 'think', to suggest that although we can provide no clear or adequate reasons for what we are saying, we do subscribe to it nevertheless. So 'I feel fairly serious' is like 'I don't know why, but I'm inclined to say I am fairly serious.'

Saying one is fairly serious is like saying 'Don't be surprised if I do it, but on the other hand don't count on it', a conjunction of two directives. On what basis do we issue these directives?

We are not always in any doubt, and in need of a basis, but sometimes we are taken aback by the question how serious we are, and one way of finding out is by addressing various questions to ourselves of the form 'What would I do if. . .?' 'If Margaret Laurence had read some of my sketches and encouraged me, would I have started working in earnest?' 'If I inherited $50,000, would I spend it on writing time, or on that ketch I dream of owning?' 'If my wife said she wouldn't mind living austerely for a while to enable me to work full time on it, would I quit my job?'

In talking here about *asking oneself* we need to get hung up on the old puzzle about who poses these questions and who answers them. They may just as well be posed by someone else; and we may volunteer answers without the questions having been put either by ourselves or anyone else. If I am asked how serious I am and after a time I say 'With some encouragement from you I would do it', that shows I am quite serious, and would be an answer to the question, if anyone had asked it, 'Would you do it if she encouraged you?', but the question need not actually have been posed. We use the expression 'ask yourself', not in preference to 'ask Melinda', not to indicate to which person the question should be addressed, but to show what kind of question we conceive it to be, namely one on which it is up to you to pronounce.

How do I know that I would. . . if. . .? Is this a prediction, and is there evidence supporting it? If the conditions mentioned in the if clause are satisfied and I do not do what the 'I would' clause declared, I do not conclude that I have made a mistake in my calculations. What I said was more like a promise or an offer than a prediction. It is an offer in the case in which I tell my wife 'I would do it if you encouraged me'. She is entitled at that point to say 'All right, it's a deal.' In the case in which I tell a third party what I would do if my wife. . . , we might call it a sub-offer. It falls a step short of offering, but having told a third party that I would quit my job if my wife. . . , I would be in almost the position I would be in had I offered, in a case in which my wife volunteers that she would be prepared to live austerely for a time. . .

We are sometimes altogether ready to make one such offer, but would baulk at making another only slightly different. How do we decide that we can say this but would not care to say that? By thinking about where we shall stand if we say *this* or say that, what advantages may accrue, what risks will be run, what pressures may be created to go one way rather than another. It is a matter of whether, when we are as clear as may be about where we would stand if we made a contemplated declaration, we can do it. We are not studying *ourselves*, to see whether a state called seriousness prevails, but testing our reactions to various *prospects*.

It is not only questions such as 'How serious are you?' that can be understood in this way. Suppose two people who usually take a trip together on their holidays are discussing where to go this year. One of them says 'One place I'd quite like to visit is Vancouver.' There will probably be a background to this contribution. She may have seen pictures, read articles or heard friends' travel reports and been intrigued. But the force of what she now says is like a promise: 'If you were to propose going to Vancouver, I would not object.' If the other person says 'I would quite like that too, but I would prefer San Francisco', that is like the offer 'If you go a bit further and actually propose Vancouver, I will not object, but if you offer me a choice between it and San Francisco, I will take the latter.' In such exchanges we are explaining our attitudes, but the explanations take the form, not of psychological reports, but of tendering offers.

Reasons for Asserting. When we say 'I say this because. . .', the 'because' is rather different from the 'because' in 'I left because he told me to.' In the latter case I suggested that we are declaring where we stand, but there we are not necessarily making any representations about the wisdom of our way of handling such situations. There it is primarily a 'this is how I am' affair and, if one is then persuaded that one has been cowardly or unwise, no pressure is thereby generated to withdraw the representation regarding why one acted as one did.

When we give reasons for an assertion, by contrast, a 'This is how I am' representation is of no interest, and we are primarily claiming that the considerations we mention do support the proposition asserted. The question 'Why do you say that?' is (not always and not entirely, but in part and sometimes) equivalent to 'Why should I agree?', and when it is so equivalent, any part of what we reply must be withdrawn if it turns out not to support the proposition asserted – not to be a reason for agreeing.

When or to the extent that the question 'Why do you say that?' is equivalent to 'Why should I agree?' there is no requirement that the reasons given should be what in fact persuaded the person giving them. It is permissible to bethink oneself of reasons on the spot, or to set out in search of reasons, and deliver them when they are found. All we are saying about any consideration tendered is that it does support what we said. Thus we are making no representation about ourselves, and the kind of problem we have often had about *what* we are saying about ourselves does not arise. If you ask for my reasons for saying it will rain tomorrow, you just want evidence about whether it will, and the fact that it is *I* who provides it is generally of no interest.

When we give reasons, we *are* of course most often asserting, not just that they *are* reasons, but they are sufficient to give us a right to believe what we have asserted; but whether we have that right, or how strong a right we have, is not a fact about ourselves, but about the collective merits of the supporting considerations.

A troublesome case however is where what someone said has turned out to be false or very implausible and he now recognizes this, and is asked why he believed it. Here there is no question 'Why should I agree?', and hence no freedom to adduce relevant considerations without regard to whether they in fact proved persuasive in one's own case; and the question seems to be a least in part biographical: 'What led you to believe this?'

In answer to this kind of question what we mostly aim to provide is face-saving: although admittedly we made a mistake, this, that and the other certainly made it look as if such and such were the case, and it was not altogether remiss of us not to have noticed or not to have given due weight to *this* and *this*. The considerations one gives as one's reasons will have to be reasons, though insufficient, or be plausibly mistakable for reasons; and whether they are such is an epistemological, not a biographical question. One would not be giving one's reasons if one said 'I had two cups of coffee that morning, and I have found that whenever I do this I tend to believe implausible propositions', even if that were true. This would assign a cause, but unless it implicitly conceded that there were no reasons, it would leave to be answered the question what reasons the speaker had.

Nevertheless in such a case if I say 'My reasons were such and such', I am saying that these are what persuaded me. We could alternatively say 'these are what *made* me believe', and it will seem a short step from this to 'These are what *caused me* to believe.' But whether this last step is justified is not so clear. Are we saying that once these considerations occurred to me, it was as only a question of time until believing happened? Or that I then believed in spite of myself? Is it supposed to be a psychological law that when that set of considerations is before a human mind, believing will occur? Or that when that set of considerations is before a mind constituted as mine then was, believing will occur? Is there any suggestion that soon after these considerations made their appearance, something happened that was identified as believing? In saying that this or that made us believe, are we

saying in effect 'I *contend that* the relation here was causal?'
When someone says 'these were my reasons', would it be in
order to ask 'Did you feel belief coming on inexorably?

I will not linger over these questions, because it is not
obvious whether they properly arise; but that this is not clear
is just the problem. These questions represent possible ways
of fleshing out what might be at issue when we wonder
whether reasons are (sometimes) causes, but since it would
not take much argument to show that none of them does
properly arise when we say 'I said that because. . .' or 'I was
persuaded by such and such considerations', it remains very
unclear what sense we are to attach to the question whether
reasons are causes.

Let me suggest an alternative picture. When we say what
our reasons were, it is not always or even very generally true
that there was a time when we were reviewing the considerations we mention. They must be considerations we *knew of* at
the time we said something or came to believe it, but knowing
something is not being currently aware of it.

In many cases where we say that something or other has
happened, we have not addressed ourselves to the question
whether this is true. I am not saying we have been indifferent
to whether it is true, but just that we altogether intelligently
take many things to be true without deliberation. Barbara tells
me she had a heated argument with George last night. I am not
sceptical, and I later pass this on as being true. It turns out to
be false and you ask why I believed it. I think for a bit and then
say 'Well, I knew things to have been quite tense between
them, and that they had been arguing quite frequently, and
Barbara seemed distressed as one might be after such a scene,
and I have never found her to be a devious person, and it
wasn't obvious what she would have to gain by deceiving me
about this.' These may be my reasons, even if I did not review
them at the time, and just took what I was told to be of course
true. In saying they were my reasons I am saying it was not
stupid of me in those circumstances, to have believed what
Barbara said, or I am saying that had these considerations (all
of which were then available to me) been assembled and cast
as an argument, they would have made it plausible to conclude that what she said was true.

Here if there was anything to serve as a cause, it would be
my being told about the altercation. Normally we believe what

people tell us. In some circumstances it is unperceptive of us to do so, and we should have known better; but the fact that it was not stupid of me to have believed what Barbara said does not show that the circumstances that made it unembarrassing to have believed her were the causes of the belief. In saying that these were reasons, I am not saying that had the circumstances been otherwise I would not in fact have believed, but that had they been otherwise it might have been stupid to believe. If I say these facts made it reasonable to believe, I am not saying that they caused the reasonability of believing, it is constituted, not caused, by these facts.

In the above example the considerations that were called reasons were not reviewed at the time something was taken to be true. Quite often however we *have* conducted a review of various facts or supposed facts, and have made a decision in the light of that review. This latter kind of case may seem more congenial to the view that reasons are causes, because the review process serves as something definite to assign as the cause, and seems to lead on immediately to something we can regard as an effect: one's taking some proposition to be true.

However if I say 'I said it (believed it, took it to be true) because. . .', it is clear now that I am not *saying* that the considerations I proceed to set forth came before my mind, *even if they did*. If someone says 'Never mind about that, just consider whether, when some facts are reviewed, and decision ensues, the process of reviewing caused the decision', my response would be that even if the relation here is causal, in saying what my reasons were, I am not saying that the relation between reviewing and deciding was causal.

Why do I harp on the question what one is saying, rather than the question what is the case? Because whether the 'because' in 'I believed it because. . .', or the 'reason' in 'The reason I believed it was. . .' are causal just is the question whether in saying these things I am alleging a causal relation to obtain – whether what one says would be false if it were found that the relation was not causal. If we found that there was a causal relation, that would not show that we were alleging it to exist in saying what our reasons were. (Here it must be remembered that the question about causality is not a question of whether, in this or that case, the review process caused the decision, but of whether, whenever we give our reasons, a causal relation of this kind obtains.)

I would be assigning a cause to my having taken what someone said to be true if I said something like 'I knew that those considerations did not at all support the truth of what she said, but I couldn't stop myself believing it, and it was clear to me that it was the facts I was mindful of that were making me believe it.' But in saying I recognized the considerations I was reviewing not to support what she said, I would be denying that they were my reasons.

We do say 'Were it not for these considerations, I would not have believed it', and this is like the causal claim, 'Had the spark plugs not been dirty, the car would have run', but the former is not a theory but a declaration. One is declaring those considerations to be, or to have been thought at the time to be, a justification for so believing.

When we say 'In view of these considerations I can only believe. . .', or '. . . I can't help believing. . .', the 'can only' and the 'can't help' may seem to express some causal necessitation, but not in every case in which we give our reasons would we make such a strong claim; and in any case the claim is clearly epistemological, not causal. We are saying that these considerations properly settle the matter, that given them it would be absurd to remain in doubt.

It is possible of course to grant all this, but say it only shows that when we give our reasons we are not noting causes. It might be urged that, even if in the ordinary course of events we have no occasion to talk about it, there may be (surely is?) a causal process at work. When we are learning to decide whether this is true or that is wise, the organism is being attuned to respond in complex ways to such stimuli as reading a report, observing an event or being asked a question, to respond in ways we call assembling relevant considerations, constructing arguments, detecting their faults, and so on; and any organism at any given time works in the way it has so far been attuned to function. There is, it might be said, epistemological discourse, in which we talk of considerations, arguments, assessments and conclusions; but behind epistemological discourse there are biological mechanisms, which function causally, orchestrate our deliberations about what is true and wise and fair, and work differently depending on the current condition of the organism orchestrating them.

Something like that may well be true, but still epistemological discourse is primary in the sense that, in teaching, we start with the knowledge or belief that *this* is sound procedure and *that* is a mistake, and tune the organism until it makes the sound moves and avoids the errors, as it were automatically. What we are interested in is whether the moves are suitable. If, as well as the slow method of teaching people, there were a method of direct organism modification, with drugs or electric shocks, and also a method of monitoring the functioning of an organism so modified, then, when we had achieved the manner of functioning we wanted, we would still not say 'The proof he gave must be sound because his brain was functioning properly.' We would not use monitoring brains as a method of evaluating arguments, but at most would conclude that an argument was likely to be sound, if it was produced by a brain functioning in the way we had found brains to behave when delivering themselves of sound arguments. This prediction would stand to be tested by checking out the argument delivered in the usual ways.

If, instead of 'These were my reasons for saying that', we say 'this is what caused me to say that', what seems to be omitted is any claim that the considerations mentioned do render the believing reputable or do in any degree support the proposition believed; and what seems to be added is something the speaker will generally know nothing about and not intend to make a claim about, namely the causal explanation of his believing. But does the *reasons are causes* thesis entail that we can substitute a suitable phrase using the word 'cause' for the word 'reasons' in sentences like 'these were my reasons'? It is not clear that this is entailed, certainly; but again that is just the problem. It is not clear what it entails, or whether there is anything interesting left for it to entail after the various possibilities that have been canvassed here have been eliminated.

What kind of instrument have we seen the word 'reasons' to be? A repetition of a now-familiar pattern may be discerned. In talking about our reasons we may seem to be recording something about ourselves, perhaps that certain thoughts came before the mind and by so appearing had an effect; but this was claimed to be an illusion, and instead the word 'reasons' was depicted as one with which we make claims, not about ourselves, but for example about how defensible it was to have believed that it would rain tomorrow. (Here I might have written '. . . how defensible it was *of me*', and thereby reintroduced an apparent representation about the speaker, but it is the defensibility of me, *or anyone else* believing, that is at issue here.) In making such claims we are taking a stand, going out on a limb, risking embarrassment if it turns out that the considerations adduced provide no support, or (more likely) insufficient support, for the proposition believed. The personal element is not entirely an illusion. It is I who hold that such and such considerations constitute reasons, and I who run the attendant risk of embarrassment; but I am not reporting doing these things, but doing them, in saying 'These are my reasons.'

There is textual support for some of this in BB 14, where Wittgenstein suggests that giving a reason for what one has done may be a justification p*ost hoc*. On the next page, in discussing the question whether reasons are causes, he says that the proposition that one's action has a certain cause is a hypothesis, to be verified by whether, in a number of cases, similar experiences were followed by similar actions. He says that by contrast the statement of one's reason is not a hypothesis. The argument appears to be that, if one proposition is a hypothesis and the other not, they cannot mean the same, and reasons cannot be causes.

1.3 Implicit expressions of attitude

In the preceding subsection I described some ways in which we explicitly enunciate attitudes. The striking thing about these ways of speaking was that, rather than reporting inner goings-on, they are themselves significant acts, of offering, taking a stand, and so on. We explain how serious we are by going on record as being prepared to do such and such if. . . , an offer on which someone may take us up.

In the present section, the place of attitudes is somewhat different. Sometimes it is part of the way a word works that, while it appears to say something just about someone else, or about ourselves at a certain time, it also expresses a current attitude of the speaker – either her attitude towards a representation she is making about another person, or an attitude towards what she has herself been doing or undergoing. In this kind of way words can be bi-valent. Not appreciating this can lead to philosophical perplexity, when we press the question what such a word says just about ourselves, or just about someone else. The following are some examples.

1.3.1 Thinking

It is clear that if someone says 'I have been thinking about your offer', what is likely to ensue is a characteristic transaction in which he may be asked whether he has decided, why he hesitates, whether there is anything further he would like to know, whether he has a counter-offer, and so on. Call such a transaction a Q-affair. While of course we do not know what will actually transpire in a Q-affair, we know in a general way some forms it may take, and the kind of demands we may have to meet as it unfolds. If we say we accept the offer, we will have to be ready to work out the further mechanics. If we turn it down, we are likely to be asked why. If we remain undecided, there may be pressure to make a counter-offer, or to say given what turns of events we might decide in favour or against, and so on.

Since a Q-affair is what naturally ensues when we say 'I have thought about your offer', we are best not to say this if we are not ready to cope with the demands typical of such transactions.

Readiness for a Q-affair need not consist in having *rehearsed* answers to questions that may be expected, whether as part of the activity of thinking about the offer, or at the later time when one is asked if one has thought about it. If one's deliberations had included the thought 'I could accept her offer if Peter would pay me what he owes me', whether one could say this as part of an ensuing Q-affair would be a matter, not of whether one had had that thought this morning in the course of one's deliberations, but of whether one was now prepared to make that commitment. (The commitment here is not: to accept the offer if Peter repays his loan, but: not to use shortage of funds as a reason for hesitating.)

How do we know whether we are prepared to make such a commitment? There is no quality that saying something to oneself sometimes has, that shows whether we could say it to the other party, thereby making it official. We sometimes know whether we could, but not on the basis of any introspective or other evidence.

Moreover it is not the case that we are ready for a Q-affair only if we have a specific plan for coping with it. We may be ready if we have handled such transactions creditably before, and simply have no need to doubt that we will manage, and will not be confused or duped by turns the business may take.

If we prove ourselves unprepared for a *Q*-affair, other people are apt to say 'I thought you said you had thought about it!'. In that way we learn not to say we have thought about an offer or a problem when we cannot at all cope with the linguistic developments that characteristically ensue when we so describe ourselves. In such ways we learn when to call the attention we have been giving the question 'thinking about it'.

For it to be in order to say 'I have thought about your offer', there must, it is true, have been times when one was for example asking oneself 'Shall I accept?', 'Where would I be if I did?', and so on. But if such efforts proved quite fruitless, if one now finds oneself, not only undecided, but with nothing in hand with which to cope with the kind of turn a *Q*-affair will take when one has declared oneself undecided – no counter-offer, no statement about why one hesitates, nothing to say about turns of events given which one might accept – if one is in that way empty-handed, one will not pronounce those efforts to have been a case of thinking about an offer.

We tend to assume that there must be characteristics just of what happened when we were trying to decide, that show whether it was thinking. We assume that we must know what these characteristics are, otherwise we would not be able to report so routinely that thinking has gone on; and we press the question what the characteristics are by which it is identified.

My suggestion, by contrast, is that we call our efforts to decide 'thinking', not on the basis of the character of what happened when we were trying to decide, but on the basis of our present readiness to cope with a *Q*-affair.

Phenomenologically indistinguishable episodes may have occurred in two cases, only one of which one would care to call thinking. The difference may lie, not in what ran through the mind at the time, but in whether one now finds oneself ready for a *Q*-affair. If I now feel quite at a loss, I will prefer to say, not that I thought about it, but that I had worried a good deal about it, or had *tried* to think about it.

This is part of the way the word 'think' works. In such cases at least, although it makes reference to what happened at some (usually) recent time, it is primarily on the basis of one's present disposition that one calls what then happened thinking, rather than worrying, trying to think, wishing one could decide, etc.

The suggestion here is not that, when we find ourselves

ready for a *Q*-affair, we infer that this morning's efforts to decide must have been a proper case of thinking, since it had suitable consequences. The supposed inference here might have some substance if thinking were advertised as a particular beneficial process that it behoved us all to learn, but that was very hard to describe, and easy to mistake – so that one could only know whether one had done it, rather than something quite like it, if, having done something in a number of cases that seemed the same, desired results ensued repeatedly. One could then reckon: what I did here must have been thinking, because it was so like what I have done in other cases, and had the effect of preparing me to discuss his offer creditably.

When we are asked 'Have you thought about my offer?', the issue is not whether something has been done that is properly called *thinking*, but just whether it is too soon to discuss the offer. We do not reply 'I believe I have', or 'All the indications are that I have.' There is room for a mistake here, but not that of wrongly supposing that what one did was thinking. If I reply 'Yes, I have', and it turns out that I have not decided, can't say why I hesitate, can't say what further information I would like, have no counter-proposal, and so on, and the other person complains 'I thought you said you had thought about it!', the objection is not that I wrongly supposed what I did to have been thinking, but that I expressed myself in a way that is correct only if one is decently prepared for a Q-affair, and I was not so prepared.

It does however *sound* as if the issue were whether something happened that is properly called thinking; and that is one of the linguistic facts that lead us to press questions like 'What is thinking?', where this means 'What distinctive act or process is it that we care about because of the benefits accruing from it, and have come to call "thinking"?'. When that seems a fair question we shall wonder whether it is possible to describe this activity and, if not, whether it can at least be identified, perhaps by the occasions on which it occurs, the purposes it serves, or the experienced similarity of what occurred in a given case to what has occurred at other times, and had similar consequences.

I will not go into the perplexities that arise if we press such questions, and will only note that the questions themselves would not arise, and we would not need either to answer them or to sigh over their unanswerability, if we appreciated the way (if I am right) 'to think' works here. If 'I have thought about it' does not say what I have done, but only that, having done something, I am in a position to discuss it, there will be no question arising of just *what* it says I have done.

A similar point can be made about the expression 'to have been thinking of (doing something)'. If I say I have been thinking of taking up hang-gliding, I will be taken (a) to remain undecided, but (b) to be quite seriously inclined – to be so disposed that with some encouragement I would quite likely go ahead with it. If it turns out that I have decided, have paid for ten lessons and am to start on Tuesday, it will be a good question why I described myself as *thinking about it*; but again if it turns out that, when you try to discourage me by harping on its perils, I impatiently dismiss your entreaties as being quite unnecessary since, for me, actually doing it is out of the question, you may object that I should have described myself, not as thinking of doing it, but perhaps as fantasizing about doing it.

Yet if one person was thinking of doing something and another was fantasizing about doing it, there need be no difference between their recent mental processes. They may both have imagined themselves soaring high over trees and fields, may both have imagined the amazement of their friends on hearing about it, may both have worked out how they might find the money to pay for it, and so on. The person who was fantasizing may have said to herself 'Of course I'm not serious about this', but so might the person who was quite seriously inclined. For her, saying this might be part of an effort to overcome the inclination to hang-glide, and so might be an indicator of how seriously inclined she was. If either of them asked 'Am I serious about this?', the question could be answered, not by a close study of the character of what had been running through their heads, but by asking themselves for example 'Would I be impatient with someone who tried to talk me into it or out of it?'. Whatever she may have felt at the times when she was entertaining various thoughts about this activity, if Mary recognized *now* that it was not something she would ever actually do, she should decline to say that she had been thinking of doing it, and prefer to say she had been entertaining herself with thoughts of doing it.

It is the attitude one wishes to express now, not the character of what has been going through one's head, that decides how to describe the episodes in which the idea of one's taking up hang-gliding has been the theme.

It is true that one can say for example 'At that time I was thinking of doing it, but later I came to see that it would be quite mad', and in that case, in spite of a present negative attitude, one describes oneself as having thought of doing it; but here the very contrast between thinking of doing it and seeing it as quite mad shows that the former description implies a serious inclination. In this example it would still not be the character of the mental process, but one's present recognition that, earlier, one would not have called it quite mad, that would lead one to describe oneself as having been thinking of doing it. It might be that one had phoned to inquire about lessons, checked one's bank balance, gone over one's budget, phoned one's life insurance agent. Remembering this would show what one's attitude had been, but would not be remembering the character or sequence of one's thoughts.

Might Wittgenstein agree? There is not much evidence, but consider:

> ... If I say I have thought – need I always be right? – What *kind* of mistake is there room for here? Are there circumstances in which one would ask: 'Was what I was doing then really thinking; am I not making a mistake?' (*PI* §328)

There is no immediate indication how Wittgenstein might have answered these various questions, but his very asking of the second of them suggests that he would answer the first in the negative; and if we take it that he also thought there were no circumstances in which one would ask if one had really been thinking, the conclusion to be drawn is that whether what one was engaged in just now was thinking is something about which we can be neither right nor wrong. That would be true if thinking were not a characteristic process, identifiable by its experienced properties, and so not capable of being identified, either correctly or incorrectly.

Wittgenstein's question what kind of mistake there is room for here suggests that indeed there is room for a mistake. If the mistake is not that of misidentifying a process, it might be that of saying 'I have thought about your offer' when quite unprepared to discuss it, or that of saying 'I have been thinking of doing such and such', when not seriously inclined to do it.

These are not mistakes about whether a characteristic process has occurred, but about the circumstances in which the word 'think' may properly be used.

There may be further textual evidence in an interpretation I would suggest of *PI* §§466–70, in which Wittgenstein asks why we think, and whether it has been found to pay? These are curious and seemingly uninteresting questions, but there might be a point of some interest in them if they were asked on the principle that only of something having a definite, specifiable character, can it be said that it has been found to pay. Then Wittgenstein might be read as suggesting that normally thinking is not such a process. (An exception would be double-checking a calculation, a definite process, that certainly can be said to pay.)

It is not helpful, when someone has a problem, to suggest thinking about it, because thinking about it is not a definite set of procedures that can be instituted if other measures fail.

It would however take more space than it may be worth, to substantiate more fully this reading of these somewhat dark passages.

1.3.2 Deciding

In some uses of the word 'decide' we can see again the pattern just illustrated, in which a putative description turns out to include a concealed expression of attitude.In many of these uses we *seem* to represent a particular kind of mental event or action as having taken place or been performed at a certain point in time, an event such that, when it has occurred, it is no longer an open question for the person in whom the event occurred, whether to do what he had been considering. His doing it is thereby settled. It is as if when we were deliberating about what to do, the plans of action considered remained mere possibilities until we did something with regard to one of them that was like pressing a button marked 'FIX' – whereupon, at least until cancellation procedures were instituted, we were so set that we would do the thing decided upon.

If I say I decided this morning, just after I heard the weather forecast, that I would patch the roof, then with some qualifications it is not an allowable move for another person to ask 'Then are you going to do it?' In saying I decided, I have already said I am going to do it. Querying whether I am going to do it is querying whether I decided. One may indeed doubt that a person will carry out the action proposed in such a case, suspecting perhaps that he will lack the courage, or be too lazy, but 'Are you going to do it?' is a question about his *intention*, and if he does not at least intend to do it, he ought not to have said he decided.

If we suspect he does not intend, we are suspecting he did not decide. The relation here is not causal or psychological, but grammatical. It is not a matter of suspecting that what he did cannot have been a properly executed case of deciding, because it failed to bring on intending. It is not that full-fledged, well-done, grade A decisions yield intentions, but rather that we only call what happened a decision if we can now profess an appropriate intention.

One may of course decide and subsequently change one's mind. It is allowable to say 'I decided, but I do not now intend' – but only in somewhat special cases. Unless one has taken some quite definite action pursuant to what one is calling a decision, like putting in an offer, making a down payment or promising, it will be puzzling why one would call what happened earlier a decision, and what happened later a change of mind, rather than saying something like 'For a time I was quite inclined. . . , but now I no longer am.' It is of course a decision if it led to some appropriate action. In other cases we shall need something to show whether it was a decision, an inclination or what; and the phenomenological character of the event itself will not show this.

It is not as if deciding were a particular kind of action or experience, and we could ascertain, just from examining what happened at a certain time, whether it constituted a decision. If saying to oneself in firm tones 'I will do it' while holding the right hand over the heart had been found almost invariably to bring it about that one did do it, and had come to be called deciding, and if we had to be careful not to do this so long as we were in any doubt about a course of action, then we might know whether we had decided independently of subsequent events. We might then treat it as a freak of nature that sometimes deciding didn't work – we decided to do something and found immediately afterwards that we couldn't honestly say we were intending to do it.

If deciding were that kind of a business, then changing one's mind might similarly be a particular action or routine that had to be gone through. One might decide to change one's mind, and have to remember actually to do it, and one might go through the procedure for a change of mind, and find that it didn't work. Then one might have to do it again, more carefully.

But if there were a procedure that had the effect of setting us quite firmly on a course, it would not be what we call deciding. We would decide whether to institute *it*, and if that decision were itself a course-setting routine, we would decide whether to institute it, and so on and on. Moreover it would make sense to say 'I decided, but it didn't work', and to say 'I think I decided, but I may not have got the procedure quite right'; but no one says these things, and we would be mystified if anyone did. We do in some moods say 'I think I've decided', but the implied doubt here is not about whether a procedure has been properly executed, or about whether the right kind of thing happened at the time the decision is supposed to have been made. We say 'I think I've decided' when we could almost say just 'I've decided', but have some slight doubts, not about whether what happened was a decision, but about the advisability of the thing we have been considering doing.

'I've decided' sounds like a report. What I am suggesting instead is that, while in many cases there is an event or an action that one is calling a decision (we can for example say 'I decided just before breakfast'), the deciding is not always thus datable but, more important, even when there is such an event or action, it is not on the basis of its properties that it is called a decision. Rather, in so describing it we are declaring ourselves firm on the topic. It is the present firmness that leads us to call the past event a decision.

Since Wittgenstein did not to my knowledge say anything about deciding, of course no textual evidence can be offered about whether he would agree with what I have been suggesting.

1.3.3 *Knowing and believing*

Earlier I argued that these words have quasi-performative aspects. In the present section the interest will be in a different feature of their use: the way, while appearing to say something just about the person said to know or believe, they also express an epistemological attitude of the person *attributing* knowledge or belief.

If I say 'Did you know that the price of milk is going up on

Monday?', the question unpacks into (a) an assertion *of mine* about the price of milk, and (b) a question 'Is this news to you?'. Since all that you are asked here is whether what I have implicitly asserted is news to you then, unless you have doubts about the truth of that assertion, all that is required for you to be entitled to say you did know is that it should not be news to you.

Here there is a somewhat complicated nest of logical relations. You do not explicitly answer the question 'Is this news to you?' If you did, you would say 'Yes', not when you had known but when you had not, and 'No', not when you had not known but when you had. And since you are explicitly answering the question 'Did you know?', you may not say you did know if for example you suspect it is not true. 'I knew it, but suspected it was not true' is not an allowable sentence, and thus in saying you knew the price of milk is going up, you are endorsing the truth of that proposition. But you need only endorse it, you need not be certain or have proof positive. It will be enough if you read this in a newspaper and did not doubt it. Then it will not be news to you, and whether it was news is what you were asked.

If I have had an argument with someone about whether there will be an election soon, and she says she knows there will, she heard it from the minister of fisheries, but I nevertheless doubt very much whether the government would be so foolish as to call an election just now, I shall be prevented from agreeing that she knows there will be an election soon. To do so would be to agree that indeed there will be one. Reporting afterwards on the discussion, I will perhaps say that Mary *believes* an election is imminent, or the she *reckons* she knows this but, in substituting these descriptions for 'Mary knows', I shall not be opining that the state called knowing does not prevail in her, only the state called believing. It is not information or surmise about her that prevents me from saying she knows, but just the fact that I have doubts whether what she says is true (and do not suspect she is lying).

I am not *inferring* that her state can't be one of knowing. It is not as if there were an identifiable state of a person we called knowing, and it had been found that it never sets in when the proposition that would be the grammatical object of that verb is not true, but that believing a proposition can set in whether or not that proposition is true. Nor is it as if, whenever a proposition ceased to be true, right away all over the world knowing it to be true ceased, to be replaced either by believing it or by knowing it to be false.

What is true here is that in attributing knowledge one is oneself endorsing the truth of the proposition said to be known, while one may attribute belief without in doing so making any commitment concerning its truth. 'It is false, but she believes it' is allowable, but 'It is false, but she knows it to be true' is not.

This is part of the way these words work, the kind of instrument they are. Appreciating this about them can relieve us of various perplexities. It seems right to say that if you know, you can't be wrong, and this may give rise to the question 'Under what conditions is it impossible that one should be wrong?' It may be difficult to see how there could be such conditions, and we may wonder whether this would entail that no one ever knows anything, or whether, to avoid that consequence, we should rewrite the above principle to read for example 'If you know, you *can hardly* be wrong.' If we made this amendment however, it would still follow that the word 'know' is misused most of the time. The person who answers 'Yes' to the Question 'Did you know the price of milk is going up?' will rarely have such grounds for believing this that he could hardly be wrong, and the person who is asked 'Do you know where she is living now?', and answers 'Yes. In Vancouver' will rarely have an answer to the objection 'Might she not have left there since you last heard?'.

What is right about 'If you know, you can't be wrong' is not that knowledge is correctly attributed only when it is impossible that the person to whom it is attributed should be wrong, but rather that it is not allowable to say 'She knew, but she was wrong.' The reason this is not allowable is that to say she knows is in part to opine that she is right, and thus one would be saying both that she is right and that she is wrong.

Similarly if we wonder what facts about her we are supposing to be different when we prefer to say that she believes, rather than knows, or knows, rather than believes, we are not reckoning with the fact that normally our choice of words here depends on no information we have about her, but only on our own opinion about the truth of the proposition she may know or believe. If one is not prepared to endorse it, one cannot say she knows, and may at most say she believes.

If the choice of word here were like a choice between various medical diagnoses, it would be surprising that there should be a *problem* what the difference is. Most of us do not know what the difference is between an attack of angina and a heart attack, but it is not a *problem* what it is. If we want to know, we just look it up, or ask a doctor.

Part of what confuses us here is that both 'She believes' and 'She knows' seem to say something just about her, and we want to know in each case *what* it says, and have difficulty finding an answer to that question that fits with the actual use of the words. This is hardly surprising when it turns out that in our thinking here, what is happening is that we are making our own opinion about the truth of a proposition into a fact about her.

1.4 Concealed metaphors

If I were to say 'She is a grasshopper and I am an ant', I would be trading knowingly on the familiar Aesop fable, as a way of saying that she is a pleasure lover who gives no thought to the future, while I am a work addict and have no time to enjoy life. The metaphors we use in such cases will often be extremely well known, and it will be clear that they are metaphors. There is a plainer way of rendering what we mean, and we do not have to scratch our heads to come up with an explanation. We shall often have begun with the wish to say the plainer thing, and reached for or hit upon the metaphor as an interesting way of saying it. No particular philosophical puzzlement is generated by these ways of speaking.

Some other turns of phrase, while comparable in important respects, are unlike this in that, although they can be recognized as metaphors if we think about it, they have come to be among the primary, plain ways of saying what we use them to say. If we use one of these expressions and someone asks what we mean, it can be like being asked what we meant when we said it was raining. We can't easily think of a better way of putting it, and may be puzzled that the question should have arisen. We may then be inclined to ask: 'Don't you speak English? If you don't understand this, how will you understand what I say by way of explaining it?' So we may be tempted to say we just meant what we said. Not that no explanation of what we meant is *possible*. In the case of 'It is raining', we could say we meant that drops of water were falling and this state of affairs was not produced in any artificial way; but this called for some effort of invention, and we might be uncertain whether the explanation quite captured what 'It is raining' says. We might feel that ability to understand the explanation was a more advanced linguistic capacity than ability to understand the sentence explained.

The following are some examples of concealed metaphors.

1.4.1 Mind, conscience and soul

We say 'My conscience has been bothering me', and likewise 'She as an agile mind', 'I have a firm intention', and 'I wondered what was going on in his head'. These sentences have come to be among the basic ways of saying what they say. We use them quite routinely, with no consciousness of being ingenious or playful, and it may require some effort of invention to explain what we mean by them, quite like the effort required to explain what we mean by 'It is raining'.

Since these turns of phrase come across in that way as plain talk, we are apt to take it that in using them we are talking about the activities, capacities or qualities of familiar things – consciences, minds, intentions; but if we ask what these objects are that we talk as if we were so familiar with, no answer is ready to hand, and it becomes puzzling for example how we can be so sure that it is our conscience that has been bothering us, if we don't seem to know what consciences are, or how we know that an intention is firm if we can't poke it, or what kind of thing we are curious about when we want to know what is going on in his head. If we find nothing we would care to call a conscience, we may wonder whether we have all been making a silly mistake in saying anyone's conscience was bothersome, or whether not just rascals and bounders, but all of us, are lacking in conscience.

Taking 'mind' as an example, we may get the hang of how these words work if we imagine that long ago there were people who spoke English much as we do, but whose vocabulary did not include the word 'mind', and that one day someone propounded a theory that people have an organ that is invisible and intangible, weightless and odourless, without which we cannot remember, imagine, think, decide, invent. This organ the theorist called 'the mind'. Imagine further that these people were not particularly inclined either to believe or to disbelieve the theory that there were minds, but it was their nature to be much intrigued by curious hypotheses, and so for a while the theory of minds was on everyone's lips, and the conception of mind, sketchy and all as it was, became well known.

One day one of these people described someone as having an agile mind. Those present were mystified and showed some consternation, and one of them asked whether the speaker believed that people actually have minds, how she knew that agility was one of the properties minds could have, and how she knew that this person's mind had that property.

She told him to calm down, she didn't know more about minds than anyone else, she just thought that if it was fancied to be by having a mind that people could do things like calculating and solving problems, there would be some difference between the minds of people who did those things quickly and inventively, and the minds of those who were slow and dull at them, and that she proposed to pretend this difference was one of agility. But, she said, to say someone has an agile mind is only intended to be a quaint way of saying that he is smart at crossword puzzles, quick to see the funny side of things, and so on.

Her friends were charmed by this, and soon were devising other turns of phrase along similar lines. It was not long before they were describing people as having lumbering minds, having something in mind, or in the back of the mind, being of two minds, being out of their minds, not in their right minds, being small-minded, and so on.

The theory of mind from which all this began being quite sketchy, predictably these expressions presupposed rather different conceptions of mind from case to case. Mind seemed to be an *agency* for the purpose of such expressions as 'an agile mind' or 'a lazy mind', but a *place* for the purposes of expressions like 'to come to mind', 'to have in mind' or 'to cross one's mind', and perhaps as a different kind of place for these than for 'to be out of one's mind' or 'not to be in one's right mind'. (In one case the place seemed to house thoughts and the like; in the other, persons.)

If these people noticed this, they were not upset by it, because they were not trying to construct a serious and coherent explanatory theory, but were only amusing themselves adding expressions to their language with which to lend variety and charm to their discourse.

Now imagine that a hundred years went by. The happiest of these constructions with the word 'mind' remained in use, but their origin was now completely forgotten, and people learned their use, not from explanations such as we imagined the inventor of the expression 'an agile mind' giving, but from noticing what kind of people were said to have what kind of minds. The mind constructions were now used routinely and without any feeling that they were quaint or amusing, and seemed to rank with 'It is raining' and 'I am hungry' as plain and basic ways of expressing oneself.

We can imagine that, in this later era, young people hearing these expressions and comparing them with for example 'That man has cirrhosis of the liver' or 'She has a broken leg' would suppose that in saying 'Mary has an agile mind', people were drawing inferences from what they observed to the existence of a state of affairs they knew something about in general, but much of the time could not directly detect; just as a broken leg may be inferred from limping and wincing, but is only rarely directly in evidence, through x-rays or autopsies. Some of the young people might thus be surprised and perplexed on finding that the older generation were as much in the dark about minds as they were – and might wonder whether the science of minds had been lost over the years, and all that had been handed down were the inferences people had learned to draw in the days when something was known of minds and their connections with people's performances in solving problems, making decisions, and so on. Sluggish performance in these matters, they might suppose, is a symptom of a lumbering mind, but what *that* is we no longer know; and it might seem to them a worthy project to reconstruct the science of minds, to find out what they are, what they are made of, how they work, what counts as being agile, which is their backside, why people never say they have something in the bottoms of their minds, what their connections are with bodies, and so on.

We can see that these inquisitive souls would be making a grave if understandable mistake, and we may suspect that it is like the mistake that has been made by dualists, parallelists, interactionists, monists, materialists. They take it that, in using the word 'mind', we are talking about something real, for sure, since some people only *seem* to have agile minds, and other people really do have them. The problem is not whether there are minds, but what a mind is. Is it the brain? Is it our thoughts, memories, feelings and intentions? Is it a different, and rarer kind of thing altogether than these?

In the story I have told, minds are imaginary entities, references to which are used to say things about people's performances, tendencies and capacities. Being imaginary, a mind could not be either identical with or distinct from a brain or a thought or anything else that is not imaginary, could not be found either to interact or fail to interact with brains or bodies or anything else, and could not be found to be made of the same kind of stuff as bodies, or an entirely different kind either.

We might indeed find that it is part of the *conception* of mind that it is immaterial, for example, just as it is part of the story of Sherlock Holmes that he lived in Baker Street; but there will not be a further question whether minds really are immaterial. That conception of mind could no more be mistaken (or right either) than Doyle could be mistaken or right about where Holmes lived – unless in his old age he forgot where he had described Holmes as living, and had to look it up.

Are there not minds? Surely some people really have agile minds, and so must have minds. Yes, some really do, that is to say we can mean it when we say this about them; but that only means that they really are quick and inventive at solving problems, at repartee, at doing crossword puzzles, and so on.

This might be the kind of point Wittgenstein was making when he said (*PI* §427) that 'While I was talking to him I did not know what was going on in his head' should be taken seriously. Most often when we say we would like to know what is going on in his head, we would like to know; but that only means we would like to know what he is thinking.

Two features of §427 muddy the water, however. The first is that Wittgenstein says 'We should really like to see into his head.' That suggests that we might cut it open or have it x-rayed if we got the chance or if it were not so dangerous; but we could take that sentence to mean that we should really like to 'know what is going on in his head', that is, that we (usually) mean it when we say this: we do really want to know what he is thinking.

The other thing that leaves Wittgenstein's meaning unclear is that 'to know what he is thinking' is itself philosophically puzzling, in a way that most other cash values of concealed metaphors are not. We are apt to backslide here and think: 'But knowing what he is thinking just is knowing what is going on in his head!'. And that is true, in the sense that the two constructions are used the same way. The trouble is that neither of them makes it clear what we want to know here. We need some explication of 'wanting to know what he is thinking' that closes off this way of backsliding, and Wittgenstein did not provide it. But it is not difficult to supply: when we say we would like to know what he is thinking, we could generally specify some questions we would like him to answer, such as why he said time is unreal: did he believe such and such, and if he did, did he suppose that the unreality of time followed from this, and so on. We would like his answers to certain questions, but we need not take his answers, if honest, to be reports of what was recently running through his mind. We just want him to show where he stands on our questions.

Wittgenstein dealt with a similar knot in our thinking in *PI* §§305-6. If you deny that there is a mental process of remembering, do you deny that anyone remembers anything? That absurd conclusion will of course follow if we have it stuck in our minds that remembering is a mental process. That connection is then like the connection between knowing what is going on in his head and knowing what he is thinking, except that the former is a deep prejudice, while the latter is correct, in the sense that the two expressions are indeed used the same way. Given that one accepts the connection in either case, one is landed in a muddle; but whereas the solution in the case of what he is thinking/what is going on in his head leaves the connection intact but provides an explanation of what both expressions mean, the solution in the other case involves denying that the word 'remember' is used to record the occurrence of a mental process.

I have not yet adduced any evidence on whether Wittgenstein subscribed to my kind of theory about the word 'mind', and in fact I know of only one place (which I will mention later) where he even hints at such a view in the specific case of this concept. However *PI* II iv can without much strain be read as treating 'soul' in this fashion. We may say 'He has a soul, you know' to someone who is demonstrating indifference to another person's feelings, and in saying this we are not expressing the belief that there are souls, and that this person has one of them. We only mean that this person too can be pained by cruel remarks. We can similarly say 'Fasting is good for the soul' or 'Her soul is in torment', even if we are not in the least inclined to think there are souls. In saying such things we trade on the picture of a soul as being responsible for sensitivities and for character, so that all we are saying is that something is character-developing, or that someone is grieving.

These points do not come out unmistakably in what Wittgenstein says, but they might be what he was hinting at when he said (*PI* II iv) 'I am not of the *opinion* that he has a soul.' He had been talking about saying of someone that he is not an automaton, which is like saying 'He has a soul, you know', and might be said if that person were being treated insensitively; and he juxtaposes the remark '"I believe he is not an automaton" just like that, so far makes no sense', with the remark 'I am not of the *opinion* that he has a soul', in such a way as to cast the two as equivalent. Hence he may be taken to be suggesting that, while one may indeed say 'He is not an automaton', there is something fishy about '*I believe* he is not an automaton'. Similarly, while one may say 'He has a soul, you know', there is something funny about 'I am of the *opinion* that he has a soul.' What is suspect about this is that we do not use the words 'to believe' or 'to be of an opinion' in connection with metaphorical expressions, or if we do we invite a literal interpretation, that generally makes no sense. (A human being can't literally be a grasshopper, and if we have only hearsay knowledge that Agatha is a pleasure-lover who takes no thought for the future, and have not ourselves confirmed it, we do not say 'I believe she is a grasshopper.' That remark might make sense however if we were watching a children's film in which grasshoppers masqueraded convincingly as human beings, and someone thought, but was not sure, that a certain character was a grasshopper. Hence ' . . . just like that, so far makes no sense' [my italics]. To say 'I believe he has a soul', we need a context, analogous to the one just described.)

So, in saying that he was not of the *opinion* that someone has a soul, Wittgenstein did not mean that he knows it, or that he is uncertain about it either. He is making a category point, that expressions of uncertainty, belief or knowledge have no place in such contexts. Saying 'He has a soul, you know' does not literally attribute a soul to him (if that were possible), but trades on the conception of a soul as being responsible for sensitivity, as a way of saying that he has sensitivities too, you know.

This reading gets some support from the final paragraph on the same page, where it is suggested that although 'In my heart I understood' is a figurative expression, one can mean it, but will not then mean that understanding took place in the heart. We may have been left to see for ourselves that similarly 'He has a soul, you know' is a figurative expression, but still one may mean it, and in meaning it we do not mean that he has a part that can continue to exist when the body disintegrates.

In *RPP* I 586 there is further confirmation of this reading in the words

> Then is it misleading to speak of a man's soul, or of his spirit? So little misleading that it is quite intelligible if I say 'My soul is tired, not just my mind.'

This is clearly a way of saying something like 'I'm not just having difficulty thinking, I'm emotionally drained', and supports the view that Wittgenstein was showing the way words sometimes work by trading on familiar conceptions, such as those of soul and mind, without presupposing that there are any such entities. (This is the place I mentioned earlier where there is an indication that Wittgenstein may be read as taking my kind of view of the word 'mind'.)

Wittgenstein may be making the same kind of point in *PI* §§423–4:

> 423. *Certainly* all these things happen in you. – And now all I ask is to understand the expression we use. – The picture is there. And I am not disputing its validity in any particular case. Only I also want to understand the application of the picture.
>
> 424. The picture is there. And I do not dispute its correctness. But what is its application? Think of the picture of blindness as a darkness in the soul or in the head of the blind man.

These sections are by no means transparent, but can be taken this way: the 'pictures' Wittgenstein is talking about are not mental pictures, such as may occur on hearing the word 'cube' or 'house', but rather such (unpictureable) conceptions as that of the mind as an agency enabling us to solve problems, or that of the soul as a part of us responsible for character, feeling and sensibility. (Wittgenstein may be using the word 'picture' here in a way like the way it is used in the colloquial expression 'Do you get the picture?'.)

The sense in which a 'picture' may be 'correct' or 'valid' is not that there are things of the kind it pictures, but rather that one may have it right about how minds are conceived if one says they enable us to solve problems and so on, and wrong if one says they are supposed to oxygenate the blood, or that when the mind departs one dies. The 'application' of these pictures is what we use them to say, for example that he is grief-stricken, if we say his soul is torment, or that she is quick and inventive, if we say she has an agile mind.

It is presumably not suggested that the 'correct' picture of blindness is of darkness in the soul. 'Blind' is not like 'soul' or 'mind'. It is not used as an indirect way of saying something about a person. Rather the suggestion probably is that we might have had the expression 'His soul is dark', as a way of saying he is blind. (But whereas the 'pictures' of minds or souls have proved fertile, enabling us to say many different things about people, darkness in the soul would be a dead-end linguistic contrivance, in that for example it would not readily enable us to say a person was blind in one eye.)

This much seems to fit these sections well enough, but the first and third sentences of §423 are admittedly awkward. What are 'all these things' that 'happen in you'? And when we read 'The picture is there', where is *that*? It reads as if 'what happens' is that a picture comes before the mind; but such pictures as that of the mind as an agency responsible for problem solving and so on are not images and do not happen, in the form of coming before the mind or in any other way. Such a picture of the mind is something we are acquainted with if we have learned English, but our knowing it is not an event. We know it day in, day out, and not more when we hear or use the word 'mind' than at other times. It is however 'there', but not in the sense that it is before the mind: rather in the sense that it is built into the language.

There is further, if somewhat indirect, textual support in the remarks in *PI* pp. 178, 204, 215 and 230 to the effect that concepts 'force themselves upon us'. One of these remarks occurs in the deliberations about the soul that I discussed, where the picture of thought in the head is said to force itself upon us; but what kind of forcing is this? The final lines of *PI* p. 178, although not specifically marked as an explanation, might provide the answer. '. . . is one conscious of using a *mere* figure? Indeed not. – It is not a figure that we choose, not a simile, yet it is a figurative expression.' Bringing these two passages together, we might get something like the following: saying 'I wondered what was going on in his head' is one of our routine, everyday, primary ways of speaking. We use it without any consciousness that we are contriving (choosing) a way of putting what we want to say. It is not like intentionally devising a simile; and we do (sometimes) really want to know what is going on in his head, (that is, we really want to know what he would say about such and such questions). But since the 'what is going on in his head' construction is such a routine way of saying what we want to know, and we use it with no consciousness of devising a figure, we may easily be led to think that it is just like wanting to know what is going on in his basement. This idea insinuates itself, forces itself upon us, by virtue of the fact that 'what is going on in his head' and 'what is going on in his basement' come across as equally routine, uncontrived ways of speaking. And (to change the metaphor somewhat), just as wanting to know what is going on in his basement implies that he has a basement, wanting to know what is going on in his mind will seem to imply that he has a mind. Similarly we say both 'Exercise is good for the heart' and 'Hard work is good for the soul' and since we would hardly say the former unless people did have hearts, whose condition can be affected by exercise, we naturally assume that we can hardly say the latter unless people do have souls. That anything is 'forced on us' here may be somewhat of an exaggeration, but something may certainly be insinuated on us unawares.

So far in this section I have only described a way in which we may see some words as working, illustrating it with the words 'mind', 'soul' and 'conscience'. Later I will suggest how some uses of a number of other words may be seen as further examples, but first I would like to call attention to a nice feature of this kind of analysis.

Although it is often (not always) behaviour tendencies or dispositions that are the *burden* of one of these ways of speaking, the concepts we are using are not therefore behavioural concepts. If saying that someone has an agile mind is a way of saying that she does certain things quickly, the latter may be a description of behaviour, but it does not follow that minds are forms or styles of behaviour. Minds are just what one might naively say they are, pieces of psychic equipment. The fact that there is no known entity that is routinely called a mind does not show that they must be something else, nor does the fact that we sometimes use allusions to minds to ascribe behavioural tendencies show that the 'something else' must be forms of behaviour. Being imaginary pieces of equipment, of course there are no minds, but that does not show that it is incorrect to say that minds are so conceived or that, to be right about what they are, we would have to say they were something else.

The following subsections will show how some other words can be seen as working in part at least, in essentially similar ways.

1.4.2 To think

Earlier I suggested one feature of the way the word 'think' sometimes works: describing what has been happening as 'thinking' implicitly expresses an attitude towards the mental episode to which we refer. There is another quite distinct aspect of this word's functioning: we sometimes make as if a process called thinking has or has not occurred, as a way of saying that what we pretend would be the consequences of its occurrence have or have not ensued. This is how I would propose interpreting the following interesting passage from *Z* 106:

> And this too could be said: Someone who *thinks* as he works will intersperse his work with *auxiliary activities.* The word 'thinking' does not now mean these auxiliary activities, just as thinking is not talking either. Although the concept 'thinking' is formed on the model of a kind of imaginary auxiliary activity.

A carpentry student will be described as thinking what she is doing if, having been taught to do so, she stops and examines the grain of a piece of wood before setting about planing it; and as not thinking what she is doing if, knowing she should do this, she fails to do it. Examining the grain is an auxiliary activity in the sense that it does not itself affect the wood, but still is something that needs to be done. Doing this however is not itself thinking: we treat doing it or failing to do it as a *consequence* of thinking or failing to think. This thinking is an antecedent auxiliary activity; but in what way can we see it as *imaginary*?

Instruction in a carpentering operation will not be incomplete if it includes no mention of thinking. We do not say 'You must do this and then this, and then you must think, and then do that', nor do we enjoin thinking all the time, never letting up. And, whereas we can instruct people in examining the grain or adjusting the plane, there is no instruction we could give in how to go about thinking. If we complain that a student was not thinking, she should not object that thinking was not one of the things she was told she must do; nor should she say 'Oh, you told me how to adjust and hold the plane, but not how to think. How is that done?'

We may complain of her not thinking even if we can see that she was going about the exercise quite attentively; and we do not say we suspect or are convinced that she wasn't thinking, and do not confirm that she wasn't by asking her. This shows that we are not as concerned as we may have appeared to be, about whether in fact she had been doing something we call thinking.

If she says that she *was* thinking, that she finds these things quite difficult, and so was thinking all the time, we will not have it out with her, suggesting that what she was doing can't have been thinking exactly, or that without noticing it she must have left off thinking for a moment. And, if we *were* to claim that it can't have been thinking exactly, we would be unable to give her a description of proper thinking, with which she might compare what she had done.

These facts would be anomalous if we were seriously alleging a failure to perform an essential auxiliary activity, but would be quite to be expected if we were making as if she had omitted or ineptly executed such an activity, as a way of saying that she had not done the job in the way she had been taught. She has had lessons in it and knows how it is done. We use the allegation that she wasn't thinking as a way of telling her that she bungled the job *without telling her in what way* – of throwing her back on the resources with which the lessons have provided her. We allege that she was not thinking as a way of *not telling her anything* about what she failed to do. She has had instruction, and should know.

People show that in some sense they know this about the word 'think' when, instead of lingering over the question whether they really were thinking, they move right on to ask

'Oh? What did I do wrong?', or when they shortly say 'Oh yes, I know! I forgot to examine the grain.'

Thinking is indeed conceived as an activity having such beneficial effects as that we remember all the steps to be taken, just as minds are conceived as pieces of equipment enabling us to calculate, make distinctions and understand arguments; but just as we draw a blank when we try to say more about this equipment itself, as distinct from what it does, we are unable to say how to perform the activity that we pretend would have resulted in creditable performance of the carpentry task.

We may want to put this inability down to the privacy and consequent ineffability of thinking; but even in our own case we cannot seriously claim to know of a form of inner exertion that we call thinking and that when successful is different, in ways we recognize but can't describe, from what it is when it is unsuccessful.

We do most often mean it when we allege that someone wasn't thinking, but what we mean is not that an indescribable but beneficial activity was not or was not competently performed, but that a task was not performed in a way the person attempting it knew it must be done. We would not say the student had not been thinking if she failed to do something we had neglected to tell her must be done.

I am not saying that thinking is always conceived as an imaginary activity, auxiliary or otherwise, but only that it is so conceived in cases of the kind I described, and perhaps some others. If I am trying hard to solve your problem, my exertions are not imaginary and will be called thinking; but if I describe Peter's remarks or Martha's gift as thoughtful, while I may appear to be saying that they had an aptness from which I conclude that they were the products of thinking, I only mean to say something about the remarks or the gift.

1.4.3 Will

Outside philosophy, there are not may ways in which the word 'will' is used in such a way as to generate the kinds of problems that we sometimes discuss, such as 'What is the will?', or 'What kind of an action is willing?' The expression 'against my will' does not generate these questions, because it clearly only means 'against my stated preference'; and, for similar reasons, neither does the expression 'last will and testament'. We do sometimes ask people to will that yonder book move across the table, but no one knows what to do by way of complying with that request. We may picture the book moving while tensing ourselves inwardly in some way, but if I reported doing this, no one would know whether I had gone about willing the movement of the book in the right way.

If we ask a person to will that his toes wiggle, he may wiggle them, and if he has no doubt that it is by willing that he makes that happen, he will suppose that he has complied with our request; but he will not be able to separate out the willing from the movements of the toes, and thereby settle the question whether he got them wiggling by willing, or in some other way.

Such expressions as 'will power' and 'strength (or weakness) of will' do suggest that there is something called the will that can be strong or weak, and so give rise to the question what a will is, but clearly that question can be discounted on the grounds that there is a concealed metaphor here: when we say that someone is weak-willed, we are not inferring from his behaviour that something called his will is substandard, but making as if that supposition were true, as a way of saying that he tends not to persist at things he finds disagreeable or difficult. We pretend that there is a part of people called the will, a piece of psychic muscle, as it were, that controls our actions, and that, when this equipment is in poor shape, it fails to overcome psychic resistance; but all we mean when we ascribe weakness of will to a person is that he tends not to overcome very much in the way of distaste or reluctance.

No doubt resoluteness and its opposite can be explained, but the explanation will not tell us what the will is, or what the difference is between a strong and a weak one, any more than, in a community in which weather reports are expressed in terms of Poseidon's moods, meteorology would tell us who Poseidon is.

Wittgenstein did not to my knowledge suggest that any of our actual uses of the word 'will' can be regarded as concealed metaphors, but he did make two of the related points I have just made. In *RPP* I 51 he said:

> How is 'will' actually used? In philosophy one is unaware of having invented a quite new use of the word...

And in *PI* §621 he can best be taken as arguing that there is no remainder called the act of willing when we subtract the fact that an arm goes up from the fact that we raise it.

1.4.4 Miscellaneous

How widely can we apply this idea of concealed metaphors? It will readily be seen how the idea would apply to the general run of what we may call faculty concepts, concepts of psychic agencies responsible for certain functions. Applications to 'soul', 'mind', 'conscience' and 'will' have been illustrated, and we could clearly go on to 'memory', and 'imagination', at least when these words are used as if in reference to a known agency, as in 'I have a poor memory', or 'She has a lively imagination'.

It is hard to think of *activity* words other than 'think' that can be viewed in this way, but attending and concentrating might be possibilities. We tend to think of these as distinctive activities having such consequences as that we become aware of things that might otherwise escape our notice, or can do things that would otherwise be too difficult; but we can no more give instruction in these activities than we can in that of thinking, and it is believable that there is nothing we know of, that we do under these descriptions; we just sometimes notice more and perform more competently in the midst of confusion than at other times.

When we say that we are able (or unable) to divide our attention between this and that, it sounds as though attention were like a beam of light that shone on the things attended to, enabling us to perceive it, a beam that sometimes could be split; but all we mean is that for example sometimes we can follow two conversations that are occurring at the same time. Saying we can divide our attention appears to explain this ability, but is in fact only another way of saying that we have it.

'You weren't concentrating!' can be seen as working in just the way 'You weren't thinking!' was described as working – as an apparent diagnosis of why a performance was substandard, which is in fact only a way of saying it *was* substandard.

'Notice' is another word that might seem to, but does not, record a special kind of mental act. 'Did you notice the small grey bird with the orange markings?' 'I saw it, but I'm not sure whether I noticed it. How does one notice?' The person who responds this way may be taking 'noticing' to be one of the acts by which one manages to see, an act that we perhaps reserve for situations in which what is to be seen is easily missed, and perhaps one that it takes practice to be able to perform successfully, like an intentional slice in golf. But this would be a misreading of the fact that we use the word 'notice', as in 'Did you notice. . .?' to express the *speaker's* recognition that the thing to be seen might easily be missed. It is not clear that there is anything taxing we do that results in our seeing easily missed things but, if there is, it would be actions such as squinting the eyes, which are not called noticing.

However perhaps noticing is best seen, not as an imaginary mental act, but as the illusion of such an act, arising from a misunderstanding. We do not say 'You weren't noticing!' in the way we say 'You weren't concentrating!', or 'You weren't thinking!'; and 'notice' is fairly clearly an achievement word, used affirmatively only if we do succeed, and regardless of what measures we may have been taking in the hope of succeeding.

A different example is that of describing something as hard to believe. In so describing anything, we may be playfully casting believing as an activity in which people can be more or less skilled, and the performance of which can be more or less taxing; but the expression is clearly only a way we have of saying that a proposition, a story or what have you, is very implausible. We talk as if, a story being implausible, only skilled believers would manage to believe it; but when faced with something 'hard to believe', we would not embark on exercises in believing until we became so good at it that the formerly hard to believe became easy. If instead we assembled corroborating evidence, we might make it quite easy to believe, but saying it is easy now would only be a way of saying the proposition to be believed is no longer so implausible. We would not mean that it can now be believed six times in a minute without exhaustion, or that it can be believed even by fairly unskilled believers.

Concealed metaphors may also be seen in some of the adjectives and adverbs we apply to psychological nouns and verbs: 'firm intention', 'fervent belief', 'burning desire'.

If, as I argued, the word 'intention' is not the name of anything, you would think there would be no adjectives describing intentions, there being nothing for them to describe. Indeed there are very few, but we do speak of firm intentions: how can that be? – What is firm will not readily disintegrate or change and is likely to endure, and so we describe an intention as firm as a form of assurance that we will not readily change our minds; but it is not upon prodding an intention, or in any other way finding it to be firm, that we describe it as firm, but rather we so describe it when we are prepared to issue a strong assurance. We do not issue the assurance on the ground that the intention is firm, we call the intention firm as a way of giving the assurance. We do not say 'My intention seems quite firm, so it looks as if you can count on my being there.' And we do not describe intentions as gooey, flabby, crumbly or anything else that they might have been instead of being firm; and that (compare not having things at the bottom or near the middle of the mind) is a sure sign that these descriptions are not fitted to the way things are. Instead, a metaphor has happened to catch on and be used, while the logical alternatives to it have not come into use.

We know what it is like for someone to plead fervently. Here the adverb describes the manner in which a familiar activity is carried out. But when people fervently believe, there is no familiar activity of believing that they will be carrying out in this manner. If Peter believes he is going to win the lottery, perhaps there is passion in his voice when he tells people this; but telling people he is going to win is not believing it. If he said it six times over he would not have believed it six times, and we do not suppose he does not believe it whenever he is not saying it.

Because people can either both say and believe, or say but not believe, we may be inclined to suppose that believing is something underlying saying, something that can be done fervently, and the fervour of which may spill over onto the saying. But none of us knows what this anterior activity is; and anything that was an activity would be intermittent, but believing is not normally intermittent and, when it is, what has happened is not that we have left off the performance of an activity, say to have lunch or to answer the telephone, and have later got back to it. We *make as if* there were something called believing that may be carried on fervently, as a way of saying that a person is deeply convinced of the truth of a proposition, and that whether it is true or not matters a great deal to him.

The words discussed in this section are instruments that work in the characteristic ways described, just as a violin works in a special way, different from that of a tuba. There might be musical instruments that produced indistinguishable sounds, although their manner of working was quite different, and there are timepieces that do just the same job, but are of an altogether different design. 'She has an agile mind' does the same job as 'she is intellectually quick and inventive', but does it in a different way. It is not the job done, but the mechanisms for doing it that we are interested in here.

These 'mechanisms', unlike the design features of scalpels, pliers, violins and ammeters, do not obey causal laws, or logical laws either. The fact that these expressions can be misused may suggest that their design enabled them to convey some things and not others, they way barometers just won't show temperature and perhaps harps just won't play extended notes; but it is only *as if* that were the case.

1.5 Words that replace behaviour

Wittgenstein thought that, just as when we are in pain, it is hard to refrain from groaning, and when we are pleased or amused we smile or laugh, when we have learned a language some utterances come as naturally as groaning, frowning or chortling, and are a sophisticated articulate form of the natural expressions of annoyance, delight, fear and so on. If the process of learning the language has brought it about that the things we say in such cases fall from our lips as naturally as groans or laughter, it can be maintained that the articulate responses have essentially the same place in our lives as the natural and, if a smile or a frown does not report anything, neither does 'How wonderful to see you!', or 'This is most annoying!'

We see this notion expressed in remarks about shuddering in *PI* p. 174, and about mourning in *PI* p. 189. Regarding shuddering, Wittgenstein seems to suggest that 'It makes me shudder', while it may sometimes be a report of a repeated occurrence not presently occurring, may sometimes itself be a shuddering reaction. If, watching someone standing on the edge of a high precipice, I say 'It makes me shudder', there may be no physical shuddering going on, but what I said as it were replaces the shuddering that might have occurred; and if in a particular case I also shudder, it may be that saying 'It makes me shudder' is not a report of the shuddering that is occurring, but rather a further reaction to the alarming thing, alongside of the physical shuddering.

Wittgenstein was making a similar suggestion when he said

When it is said in a funeral oration 'We mourn our. . .', this is surely supposed to be an expression of mourning, not to tell anything to those who are present, (*PI* p. 189)

There are problems about the application of this notion, especially about its application to the case of pain; but in some other cases it appears to me a clear and useful conception.

1.5.1. 'Pain'

In *PI* §244 Wittgenstein said

How do words *refer* to sensations?. . . Here is one possibility: words are connected with the primitive, the natural expressions of the sensation, and used in their place. A child has hurt himself and he cries; and then adults talk to him and teach him exclamations and, later, sentences. They teach the child new pain-behaviour.

'So you are saying that the word 'pain' really means crying?'– On the contrary: the verbal expression of pain replaces crying and does not describe it.

It is not perfectly clear (a) whether Wittgenstein subscribes to this 'possibility', or (b) if he does, how widely he would apply the idea to uses of a word like 'pain'; but we can see how, if some words worked in this way, certain philosophical difficulties about them might be resolved. If we were taught to say 'It's brillig!' instead of 'Yowee!', there would only *seem* to be a question *what* was brillig, or what sort of property being brillig was.

It is difficult to see how our references to yesterday's pain, or to someone else's pain, or how our description of pains as gnawing or jabbing, could be said to replace crying. When talking of yesterday's pain, there is no current crying that our words might replace; nor do we have special ways of crying or moaning that might severally be replaced by the words 'gnawing pain', 'throbbing pain', and so on. But it is at least believable that saying 'I am in terrible pain' is something people learn to do instead of crying – perhaps a way of being civilized about suffering.

I find the suggestion here implausible however, first because, when we cry, the question can always arise, 'Are you in pain?', but not when we say we are in pain, although one is supposed to substitute for the other; and secondly because, if the answer to this question is affirmative, there may be further questions about where it is and how it feels. These questions seem to mark 'I am in pain' as an assertion about something definite that is *making* us cry, whereas for Wittgenstein's suggestion to be fruitful 'I am in terrible pain' should say no more than a moan or a whimper.

If there is anything right about the idea that pain language replaces pain behaviour, I am inclined to suggest it is that we *begin* to learn the concept of pain by being taught to say 'I am in pain' instead of crying. In *PI* §244 the question was how a human being learns the names of sensations, and the answer might be taken to be in effect: 'In the case of pain, it starts this way: a child has hurt himself and he cries . . .'. Wittgenstein did not go on to say how it continues, and did not say whether he thought that in continuing, more is learned about what the word 'pain' names, but what he did say is consistent with the view that it only starts in the way he described, or that what he described is one of the ways it starts. It is consistent also with the view that, while we later learn more pain language, we do not in doing so learn more about what pain is, in the sense of learning what determines which of our disagreeable sensations are properly called pains.

Whatever Wittgenstein's view was here, and whether or not he had a good point, in the idea of words replacing behaviour we clearly have a theme that could have some philosophical uses, and I will suggest how it might apply in some cases that may be less problem-plagued.

1.5.2 'Hope'

If I hope Wendy will be at the party, I may recently have had some feelings on this subject; excitement when I thought surely she would be there, sadness when I thought perhaps she wouldn't. But it may be correct to say I so hope if nothing like that has been occurring, for example if someone tells me she may be there and this is a surprise to me and I say 'Oh, I like her. I certainly hope she will.' Here there may have been no time for excitement or sadness, and I may say that I like her without experiencing any present warm feeling or remembering conversations I have had with her. If you knew I had no relevant current thoughts or feelings, that would not entitle you to correct me when I said I hoped she would come.

One might however think that hoping can consist of various things, and that is why there has not necessarily been excitement and despair if I truthfully say I hope or have been hoping. Hope, it might be said, may take other forms, but alternating excitement and despair is one kind of hope, and is one of the things I may be recording if I say I have been hoping.

The supposition here is that 'hope' is a 'family resemblance' concept. If it were, then 'I have been hoping. . .' would be in a way like 'I bought a dog'. There the question can arise whether it was a collie, a cocker spaniel or what? But when we say we have been hoping, no one asks what kind, and that is not because, although we know there are various kinds, it is generally of very little interest which kind has been prevailing. We do not just omit to ask which kind, the way we may do in the case of the dog owner. We would not know what to make of that question.

If there were some feelings or thoughts I was recording in using this word, there might be a question *when* they had occurred. But although, because I was hoping, I felt some excitement yesterday before lunch, there is no consequent question whether some hoping occurred before lunch. If I heard a week ago of the possibility of Wendy being at the party and, if I would be pleased if she were there, I shall have been hoping for this yesterday before lunch as much as at any other recent time you care to mention, but neither continuously nor intermittently. There will be nothing we call hoping that has been happening and has not let up; and if I have from time to time had various thoughts and feelings about the possibility of seeing Wendy, I would not between times have left off hoping. If I felt some pleasurable anticipation before lunch, I would not say that a little hoping had occurred at that time.

If I happen to have had a series of conflicting reports about Wendy's whereabouts – someone says she is in Beijing, someone else that she has returned, and so on – I might hope on and off, and might date the stretches of time when I was and was not hoping; but that is not to say that something I have been experiencing ceased when I heard she is in Beijing or Capetown, and started up again when I heard that these reports were false or that she is on her way home. To be hoping, it is enough that I like her, know of the party, know she is invited, know there is a chance of her being there; and none of these conditions requires that I have any recurring thoughts or feelings.

The reason we talk at all of excitement and despair here is that, while a hoped-for event must be one that we believe would please us, there must be some uncertainty about its occurrence. It must be neither certain to occur nor certain not to occur. If someone says Wendy will certainly be there and I say I hope so, I am casting some doubt on the certainty he alleges; and if she is reported to be in Bombay and furthermore not invited, I may say 'Well I wish she could have come', but it will be strange of me to say 'Well anyway I hope she will be there.'

The reason we can wish but not hope for what we think will not happen is not that our psyches are so constructed that a characteristic feeling we call hope does not occur if we are satisfied that the event will not happen, while a rather different feeling we call wishing may occur, but because, whatever one may feel, it is incorrect to say one hopes in such a case. There is a grammatical prohibition, not a psychological impossibility here. 'I think there must be something wrong with me. I am hoping it will happen although I know it won't' might make sense if hope were an identifiable feeling. It might be clear that one was having it, and one might be surprised or alarmed that it should be occurring in those circumstances, and inclined to see a psychiatrist. But, since hope is not an identifiable feeling, one can't find oneself having it in inappropriate circumstances. What would be needed if someone said she hoped for something she knew could not happen would not be psycho-therapy, but linguistic therapy.

One could teach the use of the word 'hope' by saying it can be used if you believe there is a good chance of the hoped-for event occurring, and you would be pleased if it occurred. This might suggest that one should examine oneself for a belief and something else, perhaps an experience of pleasurable anticipation at the thought of the event's occurring. We can eliminate the first of these occasions for self-examination by recognizing that 'believe' is a 'parenthetical verb', that is, that it makes no difference if we write '. . . if (you believe) there is a good chance of the event occurring.' Hence in deciding whether to say one hopes, one might consider what information there is that would show whether the event is possible or likely, for example whether Wendy is invited, whether she is in town, whether she likes parties. The word 'believe' is in there, not because there is something else that must be taken into account, but to mark the fact that one does not have to be right in one's estimation of these chances. 'Hope' is not like 'know' in this respect. If one was wrong, one did not know, but having been wrong about the chances of an event's occurring does not entail that one did not hope; and as we have seen it is one of the uses of 'believe' to allow for the possibility of error.

What about the requirement that one would be pleased if the event occurred? It is not a prediction, based possibly on past pleasure in Wendy's company, that, if she is there, I shall be pleased. If it turned out that she was there and I was not pleased, it would not follow that I was mistaken in saying I hoped. Still, we might reckon that the prediction does not have to be *right*, it is enough if one *believes* one will be pleased. But 'I believe I shall be pleased if Wendy is there' is a more cautious utterance than 'I hope she will be there'. One may say the latter with feeling, but hardly the former, which is a sober and judicious remark.

There may well be a surge of pleasurable anticipation when we hear certain indications of what may happen (such as that Wendy may be at the party), but we are not noting such an experience of pleasure in saying we hope, nor do we conclude that a condition for saying we hope is satisfied if we feel such pleasure. If I am fond of Wendy, it is my actual fondness, not my noting of it, that leads me to say I hope she will be there. My saying this is not *based on* the fondness, but is an immediate expression of it. It is like the case in which someone says that Martha will be there and my immediate reaction is 'Oh good!', only it is complicated by the uncertainty about her presence that lurks if instead I am told 'I invited Martha, but have not heard if she is coming.' If I then say I certainly hope she will be there, I don't say it *on the grounds that* I like her, but as an immediate expression of my liking for her. The words, and the enthusiasm audible in my voice, are the same kind of phenomenon as, and not based upon, the pleasurable feeling I may have. And we say 'I hope so' here, rather than 'Oh good!' in recognition of the uncertainty about her being there.

My main point about what kind of instrument this word is, is that it is the articulate form of a pleasurable reaction to the thought of something's happening. When we hear that something we would like may happen, we may smile or do a little dance or if we have learned English say (with feeling) 'I hope so.' These responses are all so to speak on the same level. They are alternative ways in which we may give vent to our pleasure; but that is not to say that the pleasure is something distinct from the expression of it, and is made public in these ways. Nor is it to say that the smiling, dancing or saying one hopes is the pleasure. We just call these reactions 'expressions of pleasure', and those words, like so many others, can confuse us, as they will if we think: here the pleasure, there the expression of it. (Cf. *PI* §§120, 317.) To make this point, however, I had to go into another aspect of the way this word works, the fact that it is used only where there is some doubt about the occurrence of the hoped-for event. It is not just any expression of enthusiasm that the word 'hope' replaces, but only those in which it is recognized that the event about which we are enthusiastic may not happen.

Other words in this family are 'wish', 'long', 'fear' and 'dread'. When we would like an event to occur, and think it will not, we say we wish it were otherwise. When we are sure something will happen, but do not know when, and want it to occur, we say we long for it. When we do not want something to occur, but think it may happen, the word 'fear' comes into play; while when an unwanted event seems certain to happen, we say we dread it.

1.5.3 Pleasure

It can be very puzzling what pleasure is. When we are enjoying something, it is the excellence of the scenery, the flavour, the sensation, the melody that excites us, and we would be inclined to say that pleasure is a property of the phenomenon enjoyed. But there is nothing common to, and not even family resemblances among, the flavour of coffee, the Air on a G String, an evening with friends, the view of Loch Maree in the evening light, and having an orgasm, on the basis of which we might call them all pleasures: and 'That was a pleasure!' does not seem to classify the phenomenon to which one has referred, the way 'that was a mudlark' does.

Someone might say that what is common to all the things anyone calls pleasures is that she enjoys them, they give her pleasure. To say this seems to belie the fact that what we are enthusiastic about is the excellence of the tunes, the flavours, the scenes enjoyed; but, waiving that objection, we might investigate what it is to enjoy something, or to get pleasure from or be given pleasure by it. *What* is it that we get or are given here? When we enjoy a whisky sour, are we separately aware of its flavour and the pleasure it gives us? If there *is* something distinct from the flavour, that is the pleasure it gives us, and it is perhaps a sensation or a feeling, is *it* also pleasant? If the sensation is the pleasure, it seems absurd that a pleasure should be pleasant or give pleasure; yet it would be an exceptional sensation or feeling of which we could say neither that it was pleasant, neutral nor unpleasant, unless perhaps one had some special reason to rejoice in or deplore the fact that one was enjoying something. But that would be a special case; and moreover in that case too it would be puzzling what the pleasure given by the pleasure consisted in.

Some activities and events that we say are pleasant or give us pleasure, give us sensations that we like. That fact might incline us to say that, at a minimum, sensations are somehow involved in all pleasures; but this supposition would not reckon with the fact that not all pleasant things give us sensations without which they would not be found pleasant, nor with the fact that we also call the sensations we do quite often enjoy pleasant. Is there a further sensation given us by these sensations? Furthermore, if it is a difficulty that there is nothing common to skiing, visiting friends and having a shower, in virtue of which they are all called pleasures, it will similarly be a difficulty that there is nothing common to the pleasurable sensations that various activities give us.

If we say that what is common to them is that we enjoy them, that will not help, because the concept of enjoying is as opaque as that of pleasure. We can indifferently say 'I am enjoying this' or 'This is pleasant.' There would be as much reason to hold that the equivalence of these sentences shows that in saying the latter we are really saying something about ourselves, as to hold that in saying the former we are really saying something about the object enjoyed.

It might seem plausible to suppose that enjoying is pleasure-behaving or being disposed so to behave. We might have it that 'It is pleasant' means 'It gives me pleasure', and this in turn means 'It inclines me to pleasure-behave (to smile, to be eager, . . .)'; but pleasure-behaviour includes saying such things as 'My, this is pleasant!', and on the present reckoning that would come out, not as an actual expression of enthusiasm, but as a report of an inclination to express it. 'This is pleasant' would mean 'I am inclined to say this is pleasant', which would in turn mean 'I am inclined to say I am inclined to say it is pleasant', and so on.

All this perplexity arises from supposing that pleasure is for sure some distinct element in experience, either a distinct property of some objects experienced, or something distinct from and perhaps caused by the things we say we enjoy, and pressing the question *what* element it is. If we rejected this assumption about how the word works, and offered an alternative account of its working that did not generate the question what pleasure is, our problems would be shown to have been due to pressing a mistaken question.

If we could see 'I am enjoying this', 'This is delightful' and so on, not as reporting something, but either as replacing, or as having a place alongside of, smiles, chortles, eagerness and so on – that is, as being verbal forms that pleasure-behaviour may take – we would be well clear of the perplexity about what pleasure is. Just as there is no question what a smile or an eager manner reports, there would be none that 'I am enjoying this' reports. Those words would not be a report, but a sort of gurgle of pleasure.

Various details would yet have to be worked out, chief among them being perhaps what the difference is between such various expressions of enthusiasm as 'This is pleasant', 'This is delightful', 'I am ecstatic', and so on, when there are not different and clearly corresponding natural expressions of enthusiasm for which each of these can substitute. But that they are verbal forms of pleasure-behaviour is clear from the enthusiasm audible in the voice of people who use them. We would not know what to think of someone saying 'this is delightful' in a flat or a judicious tone of voice.

Might Wittgenstein agree? I know of no place where he discusses pleasure, but there are some remarks on joy, enjoyment and delight in Z 484–8, where (a) he supports the negative thesis that there is no question what joy, for example, is (see esp. §487), and (b) he relates these to emotions, like fear, through their expression (see esp. Z 485, 488). But he does not actually say that 'This is delightful' is an expression of delight, or that 'Oh, what joy!' is an expression of joy.

As we have seen, Wittgenstein does recognize similar patterns, not only in *PI* §244, but in *PI* pp. 174 and 189.

1.6 Showing by saying

If I had lost my voice for a while but my ability to speak has returned, I may show a friend that I can talk now by inquiring about the weather in Medicine Hat, or asking how my voice sounds; but if I have nothing in particular to say at the moment, I may just say 'I can talk again.' It is a peculiarity of so speaking, that anything else whatever I might have said would have done the same job, but without being another way of saying the same thing. No philosophical difficulty I know of is likely to be relieved by this particular example, but there is a pattern here that may be seen with variations elsewhere, where it may be more important to appreciate that this is how language is working. The word 'conscious', in some of its uses, is the main example I will explore.

Many of our uses of this word are not particularly puzzling. If I say I became conscious of a rumbling sound like thunder in the distance, that is a way of saying I heard something I might easily not have picked out from among other more prominent sounds I was hearing: birds singing, the wind in the trees, dogs barking, and so on. If I say I was conscious of her annoyance, I am suggesting that, although the signs of it were subtle and could easily be missed, I did not miss them. If she was complaining loudly I would hardly say I was conscious of her annoyance, just as I would not say I was conscious of a deafening clap of thunder that seemed to be right overhead. 'To be conscious of' just happens to be the turn of phrase we have for noticing things that are subtle, slight or easily missed. Perhaps there is a picture in the background of these things being there in the real world, but not being routinely replicated in another place we call consciousness, the way (in that picture) most sounds, smells and so on that we can experience at all are; but we do not need to take that picture more seriously than we do figures of speech like being broken-hearted, or having something in the back of one's mind.

It is different if the question arises; is the patient conscious? Or if the patient herself, hearing the doctor talk about her, says 'Be careful what you say, doctor, I am conscious now.' Here, because there is no mention of what the patient is conscious of, we may seem to be talking about something distinct from the sounds, pains, etc., that may be experienced, something the presence of which perhaps enables us to smell, hear or feel; and then it can be quite puzzling what this something is. It can't be entirely like having the mental stage lit, a condition on which we could see things there, because then it would be possible to say 'I am not conscious', just as one can say 'It's too dark. I can't see a thing.' A person in a coma might conceivably make the noise 'I am not conscious' but if anyone *said* this, the fact that she was saying it would show it to be false. It can't be another way of saying 'I can't hear, see, smell, feel, think. . .', because anyone who notices this is conscious.

If the doctors are conferring about the patient at her bedside and she says 'What day is it?', they will know that she is conscious. People do not ask questions or make requests unless they are conscious. (A grammatical remark.) If, instead of 'What day is it?' or 'I have an awful headache', she said 'I am conscious', they would know she was conscious, but not because she informed them of that fact, just because she had said something. We could thus regard 'I am conscious' as a way of saying something without saying anything in particular, an utterance to be used when one has no question to ask or no complaint to register, but from which conclusions can be drawn. That is the peculiar kind of linguistic instrument it is in such a case.

It is not unlike 'I am here', a remark that does not say where one is, and is fatuous when said over the telephone, but may show where one is, if other people can tell, just from hearing it, that one is in the kitchen. When asked where one was, one might have said 'Furious bananas', and thereby shown oneself to be in the kitchen. We use 'I am here' instead, not because unlike 'Furious bananas' it says where we are, but because it sounds more like a reply to the question concerning our whereabouts. That is the special way this instrument works.

But isn't 'I am conscious' more like 'I am in the kitchen'? The latter would in appropriate circumstances both say and show where the speaker was, and similarly does not 'I am conscious' both say and show that one is conscious?

'I am not in the kitchen' may both say and show that one is not in the kitchen, but 'I am not conscious' cannot both say and show that one is not conscious. 'I am in the kitchen' is an alternative to 'I am in the bedroom', but 'I am conscious' is not an alternative to 'I am in pain', or anything else. 'I am in pain' or 'I am in the bedroom' can be disbelieved, but 'I am conscious' cannot. Someone in a coma might make the noise 'I am conscious,' but uttering it could not be part of a pretence to be conscious, the way 'I am in pain' can be part of a pretence to be suffering. People who suppose one to be in the kitchen can say a good deal about what it will be like to be there, rather than in the bathroom, but people who suppose one to be conscious can say nothing about what it is like to be conscious, rather than in pain or feeling queasy. These are more of the peculiarities of the way this instrument works.

The foregoing is a free elaboration of a line of thought of which there are hints in such places as PI § 417, where we read:

> But isn't it a particular experience that occasions my saying 'I am conscious again'? – *What* experience? In what situations do we say it?

An answer to the last of these questions was given in the preceding section:

> . . . I tell someone who believes I am in a faint 'I am conscious again'. . .

This does not clearly indicate whether it is a particular experience that occasions one's saying it but, taken together with the following remarks in Z 395, 396, we can see that the intended point may be that 'I am conscious', unlike the report of an experience, cannot be mendacious, and so cannot itself be the report of an experience.

> 395. A man can pretend to be unconscious; but *conscious?*
>
> 396. . . . Is someone speaking untruth if he says to me 'I am not conscious'? (And truth, if he says it while unconscious? . . .)

The answers to these questions are presumably negative, and it is because the fact that one is speaking, or doing anything else, shows that one is conscious, that one cannot pretend, verbally or otherwise, to be conscious. If I am *pretending* to be X, I am not X. So it should be true that, if I am pretending to be conscious, I am unconscious. But if I am doing anything, including pretending, I am conscious. This is not because without consciousness I can't do anything, but because saying someone is conscious is saying he does or can do things, can hear if he is not deaf, see if he is not blind, and so on.

1.7 Variant models

There is nothing we see Wittgenstein doing more often than showing philosophical perplexity arising from not doubting that a given word will work in a way like the way an apparently similar word works – and then pressing questions that would be in order only if such an assumption were true. Frequently a puzzling word turns out to work in a way radically different from what we had supposed. As we have seen, if 'I believe…' does not report something about me, but marks a proposition true, at the same time recognizing that the question of its truth is not past doubting, the question what it reports about me will not arise.

Here the difference between what we may have assumed and what we find is very marked, and easily grasped; but in some cases the differences are fine, but no less important for that. Then however they may be quite difficult to appreciate. (Cf. *Z* 349: 'It is difficult to deviate from an old line of thought *just a little.*')

The latter kind of case is what I am calling a 'variant model'. I believe we are confronted with a variant model of the workings of a word in Wittgenstein's handling of the word 'pain', and that is what I am about to show. I think I stand alone in my interpretation of Wittgenstein on this topic, but I am not for that reason in much doubt about whether I am right.

With many of the words I have been reviewing, a pattern has emerged in which it turns out to be an illusion that the word records the existence of a characteristic state of affairs or the occurrence of a characteristic event or process or the performance of a characteristic act; and instead, I have argued, words may work in a variety of other ways, among them inviting a certain kind of discussion, taking a certain kind of plunge, and so on. That pattern will hardly be repeated in the case of the word 'pain'. Whereas we are at a loss what phenomenon to focus our attention on as being our belief that smoking is bad for one's health, or our intention to give it up, we do not at all have that problem in the case of the present jabbing pain in the shoulder, and we cannot make it out to be an illusion that the word 'pain' refers to something. (Cf. *PI* §296.)

There are problems however. It can seem puzzling how we identify a sensation as a pain, and not something else. Objects are usually identified by their properties ('If it is like so and like so, it is a mosquito'), but we do not seem to be able to describe pains, at least not in a parallel way. We do describe them as streaking, jabbing, throbbing, gnawing, but these words seem to record the behaviour of something, and do not describe the something that is behaving that way.

Just as many different insects might swoop, buzz or flutter, and we would not know something was a mosquito just because it was swooping or buzzing, so many sensations might streak, gnaw or throb. Itches, tickles and sensations of warmth do not in fact streak or gnaw, but sensations other than pains throb, and there might have been others that streak or gnaw. It is true that mosquitoes buzz in a very characteristic way, and we often know just from the sound they make that there is a mosquito around, but still this supposition stands to be verified by getting a look at the buzzing thing itself. We have no parallel way of verifying the supposition that what is streaking or gnawing is a pain.

Here one might be inclined to suggest that, although sure enough words fail us when we try to say how we know it is a pain and not something else that is jabbing or throbbing, we do know. We know because the indescribable feel of a pain is so like the feel of sensations we have called pains in the past. But that of course only raises the question how we knew the sensations we had in the past were pains.

It might be thought that there is no problem here: if we can learn to re-identify colours, in spite of there being no other description of them than 'blue', 'red', and so on, just through their similarity to what has been called blue or red in the past, can we not in the same fashion re-identify pains? But learning colour language is different. Another person can see the coloured object I am looking at, and tell me 'We call that colour "blue", but another person cannot tell me, at least not on the basis of having identified its indescribable quality, that the sensation I am having is called a pain.

In fact it is not at all clear that we do identify sensations as pains by the quality of what streaks or gnaws (or in any other way). We never think 'This must be a pain, it's so like what I have had before'; and if we had an excruciating sensation that felt quite different from what we had been calling pains, we would not know what to think about whether pains varied in quality more than we had supposed, or whether this sensation, being so different, was not a pain, but something else.

When that *kind* of question comes up elsewhere, some people know the answer. A distinction is regularly made, that other people know and one has oneself yet to learn. But in the case of pain everyone is equally baffled by questions like this, and that shows there is no answer, and that the quality of the sensation is not treated as essential to its being a pain.

But isn't it essential to anything's being a pain that it be disagreeable, and is that not a quality that sensations may have, in virtue of which they are called pains? The adjective 'disagreeable', by modifying the noun 'sensation', may appear to describe a quality that some sensations have, but in fact it is used to express a reaction to some sensations: people abhor them, want to be rid of them. And whereas if I abhor a sound, I may be able to say what I dislike about it, the question what I dislike so much about pains leaves me (and everyone else) at a loss.

If some sensations had a quality that I hated, it would be conceivable that you should have a sensation having that quality and like it, or not mind it; but it is not the case that,whereas people's tastes differ in many things, we are at one in abhorring pain. Rather, we do not call anything a pain unless we (in some measure) abhor it.

What confuses us here is this somewhat unusual relation between word and object. There is an object, all right. It is perhaps in the shoulder, and frightful; and we call it a pain; but we take it that just as there are properties that what buzzes has, that will show whether it is a mosquito, there will be properties that what jabs or throbs has, that will show whether it is a pain. Not being able to say what these properties are in the case of pain, but still demanding that there must be such, we are driven to say that we never know whether another person is in pain.

Our thought here is not that she may not be suffering, but that the sensation she is finding so disagreeable may not have the properties that make a sensation a pain. As long as we do not doubt that pain will have defining properties, we put our inability to say what they are down to their indescribability, and put their indescribability in turn down to their privacy. It is as if a proper pain were fiery red in colour, and perceived by an inward eye, while the only colours we saw in the real world and could learn the names of were altogether unlike it, greys, greens and blues. We could not describe pains using the common colour language, and hence there would be no way of telling whether another person's disagreeable sensations were fiery red, and therefore pains.

What I am suggesting in place of this is that, if sensations have something corresponding in the above analogy to colours, still we do not call a sensation a pain in view of its 'colour'. Rather we say it is a pain if we abhor it, if having it we wince and moan (or, if we are stoical, if we have to restrain the inclination to do so). If there were a drug that left the sensation unchanged, but made us quite indifferent to it, we would not know what to say about whether we were still in pain when under the drug's influence.

I am not saying that a pain is a sensation plus an abhorrence reaction. The pain is just the sensation. It is perhaps in the elbow, while the wincing is in the face, and the disposition to wince is not easily locatable. There is not a larger entity of this kind that does have properties by which it can be identified, and we do not even exactly identify a sensation as a pain by the fact that we abhor it. We do not ask 'Is this sensation a pain?', and answer 'It must be, since I abhor it'.

Can't people like pain? Don't masochists like it? If a sensation is not abhorrent, masochists do not want it. They want to suffer, and rejoice in the ghastliness of pains.

There is a distinctive relation here between word and object that we might regard as a feature of the way the word 'pain' works, or part of an answer to the question what kind of instrument it is. It is through not appreciating the difference between the way this word works and the more usual relation between words and what they name – through expecting the usual relation to hold – that we come to say such things as that we never know if another person is in pain. That conclusion emerges only if we assume that pains, like mosquitoes, must be identified by their properties.

By recognizing that there *is* both word and object here, they are just related in a rather special way, we avoid occasioning the protest 'But there is *something* there all the same accompanying my cry of pain. . . and this something is what is important – and frightful.' (*PI* §296.)

Would Wittgenstein agree with this? The main evidence on this appears to me to be:

1. In *PI* §244 he asks how the relation between the name and the thing named is set up here, or how human beings learn the meaning of the names of sensations. In this passage he displays no scepticism about whether such a connection is set up. He goes right on to give one possible way, and suggests

another way in §288.

2. In §261, when it is denied that 'S' is the name of a sensation, we have to remember that this is a quite different thesis from the denial that the word 'pain' is the name of a sensation. 'S' was introduced in the diary example in §258, which was set in the very special circumstances laid down in §256, in which there is no natural expression for the sensation. Those are not the circumstances in which the word 'pain' is used or learned.

3. In §256, 283 and 288, where problems arise from subtracting the natural expression of pain, it is implied that the natural expression has some essential role (as it does in my suggestion), even if it is not perfectly clear there or elsewhere what that role is.

4. In §271-4 the problem clearly is that we are wanting to call a sensation a pain only if it has in itself some property by which it is identified, corresponding in one analogy I used to the 'colour' of pains.

5. In §290, when Wittgenstein says we do not identify our sensations by criteria, I take him to mean that we do not check them over, to see if they have all the right properties to be pains. I take him also to hold that we do not identify them in some other way: we do not *identify* them. Concluding 'Yes, this is a pain' would be the end of a language-game in which we asked 'Has it *a*?', 'Has it *b*?', and so on; but when someone says she is in pain, we do not say 'Are you sure? Have you checked out your sensation carefully?' And this is not because we are so trusting or so sympathetic that we do not want to waste time with these technical points: none of us would know what questions to ask, to determine whether someone's sensation was a pain.

6. The last paragraph of §293, which reads 'That is to say: if we construe the grammar of the expression of sensation on the model of "object and designation", the object drops out of consideration as irrelevant', may seem to be counter-evidence. (It should of course read 'object and designator'.) Wittgenstein seems to be saying that an unacceptable consequence, the object dropping out as irrelevant, ensues if, as I have done, we say that there is a word and something it designates. But it would not be outrageous to insert the word 'usual' in front of 'model', yielding 'on the usual model of "object and designator"', and then Wittgenstein's point might

be that the trouble lies, not in taking it that there is an object designated, but in a hasty assumption about the relation between word and object. He does seem to imply that there *is* an object designated, when he treats it as absurd that the object should 'drop out of consideration as irrelevant'.

7. In *PI* §304 Wittgenstein says that pain is not a something, and not a nothing either. It is far from uncontroversial what he might have meant by this, but it is not absurd to suggest that being 'a something' is being a typical object identifiable by its properties: a mosquito, a waltz or a poem. We can't doubt in an average real case that a person is in pain (*PI* §303), but when we ask 'How do I know that what he has is a pain, exactly?', a doubt seems to have arisen. The question presupposes that pains, like waltzes and poems, are 'somethings', identifiable by their properties – that what he has, not having the required properties, might not be a pain.

1.8 Words and their objects

In trying to see how we can look on words as instruments, as hard a problem as any will be how this can be done in a way that is philosophically interesting for words such as 'house', 'dog', 'skip', 'run', 'win', 'government', 'yellow', 'triangular' or 'slowly'.

A first thought might be that the idea of family resemblances brings out something that is instrument-like, in being of some complexity. The criss-crossing and overlapping resemblances between various things called by the same name might be thought of as a complicated instrument by which we identify games, houses, checkmates or what have you; but, if there is a device here, it is very unlike any ordinary instrument in being extremely uncoordinated in its design; and in any case it is doubtful whether Wittgenstein intended the network of family resemblances to be a way of deciding whether something is a such and such, rather than just a way of relieving one's distress on finding that there is not always any one thing in common between everything that goes by the same name.

The way we tell whether something is a game is not by whether it sufficiently resembles chess, blackjack or lacrosse, but by whether it is standardly called a game. There are more resemblances between hockey and figure skating than there are between chess and most other games, and yet hockey is a game and figure skating is not. The Olympic Games do include figure skating, but most of the activities included in the Olympic Games are not games either. We do not say 'Let's have a game of 100 metre dash' and, if someone suggests playing a game, no one responds 'How about boxing?'.

We have a model for the criteriology of class membership in the case of the members of a family. John, Beth and Mary are siblings. John's eyes are like Beth's, and he and Mary are of the same build; but Graham is not a blood relation and looks more like Beth than John or Mary do; and what shows who are the siblings is not the resemblances, but which people have the same parents. Similarly there is a non-family-resemblance criterion of what is a game or a dance. It is for example whether people smile if one lists philosophy with old maid, backgammon and rugger as games. If someone says philosophy is a game, he is not noting a fact of English usage, but expressing an opinion or an attitude.

Another possible way of seeing general words as instruments is this: Wittgenstein sometimes (for example *PI* §142, 242; pp. 56, 225, 230; *Z* 331–93) discussed the question of the relation between language and the world, such questions as whether it is the business of concepts to reflect accurately the way things are, whether some of our concepts might inaccurately do this, whether we must extend the application of a concept wherever we find a similarity between what we have been calling Xes and some further phenomenon, and in virtue of what kinds of change our concepts will need revising.

Some of his views on these questions appear to be:

1. Concepts are the expression of our interest and direct our interest (*PI* §570; see also *Z* 580). He does not say, but presumably would say, that the concepts of which he is speaking are not generally concepts of some interest. Rather what is included in and excluded from a concept may reflect some interest. A community might divide non-botanical, non-human living things according to whether they were benign, calling anything benign an animal and anything hostile a beast. If someone in that community said 'Isn't a butterfly too different from a dog for them both to be called animals, and isn't a wolf so like a dog that if one of them is an animal, the other should be too?', they might reply 'We are not interested in those similarities and differences. Butterflies and dogs are benign and wolves are hostile. That's all we need to know.'

Their interests would be directed by concepts if they were anxious to add to or revise their lists of beasts or of animals. If an insect previously thought to be benign were found to bite, they would add it to their list of beasts, but in doing so they would not be changing the concept of a beast as a hostile non-vegetable, non-human living thing. Whether they continued to make this classification, might for one thing depend on whether there was a change in their ways of living or their tastes: they might cease to be animal herders, or cease to enjoy the company of dogs, cats, budgies. Then they might no longer care whether a certain living thing was hostile, and might get out of the way of distinguishing animals from beasts. This would show that in a broad sense their concept would be related to their nature, and so to the way things are, but still the concepts 'animal' and 'beast' would not be concepts *of* their nature, and would not be shown to have been *incorrect* by this change in their nature.

2. Some concepts are applicable only given certain conditions, but are not concepts of those conditions. Nevertheless if the conditions were known to have changed we would be all at sea, and no longer know how to apply the concepts. We would be thrown into confusion about geometrical demonstrations, for example, if we thought diagrams had taken to changing unperceived, or if we developed a distrust of our own or other people's memories (*PI* p. 225); and the concept of a kilogram of cheese as the amount that will balance the scale if *this* weight is in the other pan would come unhinged if lumps of cheese suddenly grew or shrank for no obvious reason (*PI* §142). The explication of the concept of weighing does not involve mentioning that things weighed should change size only in regular ways, but if this were not true we would not have the concept (see also *Z* 350, 393).

3. Were it not the case that people readily learned to distinguish red from blue, and to call various shades of red or blue 'red' or 'blue', if they often thought they had learned the system and went away insistently calling blue what others called yellow and still others brown, there would be no colour language; but still, in saying this is blue or that is red, we are not saying anything about this condition on which it makes sense to say such things (*Z* 351, 355, 366, 393). In describing the colours of things we are as it were putting our acquired discerning equipment to work doing some of the things it will

do when in good shape but, if some equipment when in good shape makes colour discernments, it is not in doing so advertising to the shape it is in. (We have acquired colour-discerning equipment when the colour judgments we make are much about the same as other members of the linguistic community; but, in saying how blue the sky is, we are not saying people will call this blue, but just for our own part so describing it.)

4. The question 'Am I applying this word correctly?' makes sense if it is taken to be a question whether I do it the way the linguistic community does, but it is not clear if the question whether the linguistic community applies it correctly makes sense. It does if it is a question whether a principle of classification the community has yields the judgment that this is a such and such (for example 'Is this organism an "animal"?', when we have the principle that the benign will be called animals); but if we ask 'Are we right in having that principle?', we shall not have any principles ready-made with which that question might be answered. And if we devise some principles for this job, they will better have to do with importance, convenience, learnability, than with the nature of the beings to which 'beast' and 'animal' are applied.

Suppose it were noticed that sometimes some members of the same litter are benign and others hostile and someone therefore suggested that it only makes for confusion to call some of them animals and others beasts, when there is no other relevant difference than that some are benign and others hostile.

The imagined distinction would indeed be confusing if most of the community's other classifications of living things were based on features that were genetically invariant; but (a) a community is imaginable in which no interest was taken in that kind of feature; (b) even in a community in which there was also that kind of classification, people could say 'Yes, it can be confusing, but for the most part we function quite satisfactorily with the system we have and, when confusion does arise, it is cleared away easily enough by pointing out that "animal" and "beast" are a different kind of word from "collie" and "bulldog"'; and (c) the objection here *is* the fact that it can be confusing, not the claim that it is wrong – that it incorrectly mirrors reality – to have classifications based on anything but features that are genetically invariant.

If a zoologist were proceeding on the genetic invariance

principle in classifying living things, it would certainly be a mistake to assign the benign and the hostile in a litter to different categories, but it is only within such a stated classificatory guideline that such a move would be a mistake, and there is no necessity that we should adopt one such system rather than another. Nor are the classifications we ordinarily make always based on any hardened set of classificatory principles.

In *Z* 391 Wittgenstein said

> I really want to say that scruples in thinking begin with (have their roots in) instinct. Or again: a language-game does not have its origin in *consideration*. Consideration is part of a language-game.
>
> And that is why a concept is in its element within the language-game.

Among the 'scruples' I take him to be talking about would be for example the case I imagined in which someone reviews the question whether such and such is properly called an 'animal'.

What he means by 'instinct' is hard to say with confidence, but an interpretive possibility may be derived from *Z* 121, where there is the example of a man who knows his way around a city perfectly, but is quite incapable of drawing a map. When he tries, he gets it completely wrong. Wittgenstein adds: '(Our concept of "instinct").' Presumably the 'instinct' here is his ability to find his way around the city without a map and, unlike the usual conception, is not a matter of his doing something intelligent without having learned to do it, but rather of his doing something comprehending without being able to say how he does it, and whether or not it is something he has learned. (In the example he no doubt *would* have learned his way around the city.)

Applying this to *Z* 391, our understanding of the language-game would be something 'instinctive'. It may be *possible* to formulate what we know, just as it is possible to draw a map of the city, but we can play the classificatory language-game without being able to say how it is played, just as we can get around town without being able to draw a map.

Now if there is to be a way of dealing with our 'scruples', there must *be* a classificatory language-game we are playing. Except as part of a language-game, when we have scruples about our words, we are floundering, not carrying out any manageable operation. (Thus 'Consideration is part of a language-game.' [Z 391]) What we find, however, reverting to the 'beast/animal' example, is that while we can have scruples about whether to call this being a beast, those are part of a language-game in which if anything is hostile it is called a beast. But it is not *that* kind of scruple that figures in the philosophical anxiety, but rather a question *whether to play* the beast/animal language-game. And it is not clear whether there is a further language-game in which this question can be considered. We are perhaps playing such a game if we allege that to have the beast/animal language-game alongside the dog/cat/budgie/wolf/bear. . . language-game is too confusing; but it is not clear whether there is such an established game, or how it works.

We seem thus to be left having to contrive a language-game in which to conduct this philosophical business, and about this prospect Wittgenstein says that a language-game does not have its origin in consideration. I take him to mean here that we run out of anterior language-games in which to devise or alter a language-game, as distinct from reconsidering some of the moves we may have been making as part of it. The foundational language-game for any operation of considering will be one that is 'in place', and it need not have been devised, but may have come to exist in some undeliberate way, and will survive for the kind of reasons that poker or hockey survive. It suits the human beings who play it.

5. In some cases, quite independently of language, reality seems to divide itself up in such palpable ways that it is natural to suppose that language has been constructed in such away as to mirror these obvious divisions. The walls of the room, by being perpendicular, mark themselves off from the ceiling or the floor, and the ceiling, being above, is marked off from the floor, which is below. The book and the desk mark themselves off from one another and from the floor by being independently portable, and the parts of the French flag are unmistakably different from one another.

No one, I hope, is going to say that without language we would never notice these differences, or to deny that in fact some of our words reflect such differences. But the idea that language should properly mirror reality would seem to entail both that a language stood in need of revision if reality included any noticeable difference that was not reflected in a stock word or expression in the language, and also that, corresponding to any word of an appropriate type, there is a difference of a kind that might strike anyone, whether or not they know the word or stock expression that marks it. [Notes on this: (i) I say 'a stock expression' because of course we can always contrive a description of anything. If we did not have separate words for the two horizontal parts of a room, we could ask someone to paint the ceiling using the words 'the horizontal part that is overhead'. It might be made an issue whether in fact it is always possible to devise descriptions in that way, but the question would be made curious by the fact that, to give an example of something we could not describe, we would have to describe it. Can we describe the smell of coffee? Isn't the expression 'the smell of coffee' richly descriptive? (Cf. *PI* §610). (ii) I say 'of an appropriate type' as a short way of confining the discussion to words such as 'wall', 'ceiling', 'book', 'desk', 'red', 'round'. With anything that marks itself off from other things less palpably, it becomes plausible to say that we learn to distinguish it by learning the language.]

Suppose there are four characteristically different designs of telephone. Each is very common, so that people come to be able to recognize them instantly, and can say 'That's the kind I have', 'That's the kind Sheila has' and so on. People, let us suppose, will straight away recognize an imitation as not being quite authentic, and could model any of them in clay convincingly or well enough that one could tell which kind was being modelled. Would it be a deficiency in the language if there were no word for the various designs? It might, if people had strong preferences for one over another, or if they otherwise became a frequent topic of conversation; but, if people were quite indifferent to the differences, the fact that there were differences would not itself require that there should be words to mark them.

Or suppose that the only reds in the world were in paintings, which were always done with one hue shading into another, and suppose further that people acquired such a command of words like 'pink', 'scarlet', 'maroon' and 'orange' that, if asked to draw a line marking the limits of what they would call 'pink' in a certain coloured print, their lines would all be drawn in about the same place. Would that not be a case in which there was a word having a definite application, but corresponding to it there was no obvious place where a colour left off? And isn't our colour language more like this than would appear from such examples as that of the French flag? In those examples we are struck by the sharpness of the line between the white and the red or the blue, but the line will be just as sharp if the colour bordering the white is one we would not just flatly call red, and our recognition that it is not quite red has nothing to do with the sharpness of the line between it and the white. We are in a way like the people in *Z* 368 who have learned a notation in which to make very fine colour discriminations. The differences are obvious to them when they have learned this notation. Without what they have learned, it might be obvious that there are differences, but what they are would not be obvious. What *we* have learned is not so highly articulated as their discriminations, but when shown an area in which red shades off into white, if we mark the part of that area that it would be correct to call pink, we are, like them, exercising an acquired ability that does not (could not) reflect the fact that that part *is* pink. What could that mean, other than that the community so describes it?

6. That this is pink and that is green will be obvious when we have learned colour language, and it will be obvious too that such and such objects are the same colour even if we do not have a word for their colour; but we are making a mistake if we think we could have constructed our colour language just by giving names to what is thus obvious. Without language it is not obvious that *these* shades are all pink, whereas *that* is rather too dark to be called pink, and *this* would best be called muddy pink. It is pink, all right, but requires an adjective, while these others are pink *sans phrase* in spite of their differences.)

Without language it is not clear that blue, yellow and red are all colours. When Wittgenstein asks why we might not group red, green and circular together (*Z* 331), he is presumably not suggesting that actually we might, and just wants to get straight why we do not. If we say 'Because red and green are colours, and circularity is not', we are forgetting that this could not be said at the point at which the concept of colour was being set up. If we say 'Because there is a similarity between red and blue, and not between red or blue and circularity', we are forgetting that red and blue are, unlike green and turquoise perhaps, entirely dissimilar. We could say they resemble one another in being colours, but that just means that we call them both colours. They are not alike in having the noticeable property of being a colour.

We might be on the right track if we said that circles can be red or blue, but blues can't be red, or reds blue, and that, at least in the sense that we do not say 'The book is a circular blue', blues and reds can't be circular; but these are not discoveries about reds, blues and circles. The proposition 'Blue reds do not exist' is not like the proposition 'Cats that fetch sticks do not exist.' We know what would count as a stick-fetching cat, but not what would count as a blue that was red. Isn't the fact of the matter not that reds, blues, and circles are too dissimilar to be grouped together, but that there is as it were a rule that if anything is called red it may not be called blue, but no rule that if something is called round it may not be called blue? This is part of our colour system. The system does not reside in the nature of colours (Z 357).

Do not at least some parts of it 'reside in the nature of colours'? Is there not a visible similarity between various shades of red, or blue, or green? Well, we can *see* that there is a touch of red in this yellow, but cannot see the touch of red in this green (Z 365), but that does not show that there is something common to reddish yellow and pink for example. We could not produce a sample of what is in common here, the way we can produce a sample of the colour, patches of which are to be seen in both yonder paintings (*PI* §72).

In Z 365, having said that we are not able to recognize straight off a colour that has come about by mixing red and green as having been produced in that way, Wittgenstein goes on to ask '(But what does "straight off" signify here?)', and in Z 359 he has suggested that this ability when it exists may be the result of experience and education.

When he said in that section that it does not matter whether it is the result of experience and education, his point presumably was that, still, with that experience we do recognize the red in a reddish yellow straight off. The origin of the ability may matter from another point of view, however, in that if this recognizing requires experience and education, it will be at least doubtful whether it 'lies in' our nature or in the nature of the colours, especially in view of the fact that reddish yellow is so very different from scarlet. Even if with a microscope, we could see specks of red in reddish yellow, but not in olive green, that would not show that the red was visible without a microscope (cf. *PI* §171), but only that the colour impression is produced in a different way when red and green are mixed from how it is produced when red and yellow are mixed. (I am not saying this is in fact the case, just following through on the present hypothesis.)

How might it come to be obvious to us that certain objects were a reddish colour, while we did not see olive green as being reddish? In the *Brown Book*, p. 134, Wittgenstein, though not clearly addressing himself to this question, suggests something that might lead us to an answer. He says that we might have been shown various patches of colour and trained to answer the question what they have in common by pointing to a primary colour. Since standard red is so different from reddish yellow, in the early stages of this training we would perhaps have no idea what primary colour to point to but, after having been told the answer in various cases, and having been corrected in further cases when asked to decide on our own about colours not covered in the instruction, giving the right answer, that is, the answer the teachers would give, might come to be automatic, and seem obvious.

Part of what we would learn here would be *not to point to anything* in the case of red and blue, or in the case of orange and olive green. Under this training it would not come to be obvious that olive green was a reddish colour; and it would be the training, not the nature of olive green, that brought about this result.

'But wouldn't the training take the form it did because olive green is not a visibly reddish colour? Wouldn't the teachers be wanting the students to learn to speak in ways that reflect the way things are?' No, all we need suppose is that the teachers having had the same training, had come to find it obvious that olive green was not a reddish colour, and wanted to pass on the language they had learned.

'But why would this language have taken this shape in the first place? Why would there have been this distinction between various colours, all of which had red in their mix, but only some of which are called reddish?' Couldn't we answer 'Who knows?'? (That answer would be a way of expressing the view that it does not matter how we came to make the distinction, what matters is whether individuals make it the way the linguistic community does. There is no need to deny that there will be some cases in which a distinction is pre-linguistically obvious, and language reflects this fact. That would not support the general thesis that it is the duty of language to mirror reality.)

7. If we think we can examine the phenomena and tailor our concepts to them, we must reckon with a point of Wittgenstein's in *PI* p. 231. In the course of a discussion of whether introspection might show if remembering has experiential content, he says that introspection 'cannot shew me what the word "to remember" means, and hence *where* to look for a content'.

The proposition 'Remembering has no experiential content' might mean either 'When one looks at the phenomenon of remembering, one finds it to be empty of experiential content', or 'The concept of remembering is not that of an experience.' It is the latter I suggest Wittgenstein means. If we (mistakenly) took this to be correct only if the former is true, that is if we took it that the concept of remembering should reflect what remembering is, and that we would have to examine remembering to see if it has experiential content. Wittgenstein's point is that what to examine with a view to discovering whether there is experiential content (or whether there is anything to examine) *is already prescribed by the concept.*

Whether the concept of remembering is that of an experience would be shown, not by introspection, but by studying grammar: by whether we take anything about the character of the experience we are having to show that we are remembering, or whether if we experienced nothing in particular and just said 'I remember her saying . . .', that would show that we did not remember. But we do not say 'That was not remembering. It was not vivid enough (or steady enough or any other word describing an experience)', nor do we say 'If you didn't experience anything at the time you say remembering occurred, you were not remembering.'

These points go together to make up a picture of the use of general words in which they are not tailored to the way things are, but rather divide the world up in ways that interest us, or at least in ways we learn from the community, ways that, whatever their origins, have survived because they suited human beings.

Such sometime principles of classification as that if A and

B are similar in such and such a respect, we should call them by the same name, do operate, as in the example of revising a community's list of 'beasts', but they operate only when or if the similarity matters to us, and would not prevent listing mosquitoes and bears as beasts in spite of their dissimilarity; and what counts as a similarity will often be a matter of what we have been taught to call similar.

How can these words be seen as instruments? I have been suggesting ways in which general words, like instruments, have their own several ways of functioning, and are related in various ways to facts of nature, including facts of our nature, but do not, in being used, say anything about these facts. The invitation is to look and see in detail how they work: not what they do, but whether they all do something in the same sense and, for anything a given word does, how it does it. (This instrument tells time, and that is a very different sort of function from recording temperature or making an incision; and various time-telling instruments or temperature-recording instruments may work in entirely different ways.)

A whale is a mammal and red is a colour, but saying the latter is saying that 'red' is a word like 'green', 'mauve' or 'brown', while saying the former is not saying that 'whale' is a word like 'dog', 'horse' or 'gerbil'. We can say what features a whale has in virtue of which it is called a mammal, but not what features red has in virtue of which it is called a colour.

Some people say that white and black are not colours. It is not clear whether they are right about this but, if they were, for example if, in buying a can of paint, 'black' was not one of the answers to the question 'What colour do you want?', and shopkeepers asked rather 'What colour do you want, or do you want black or white?', we could discover that, contrary to what we might have supposed, black was not a colour; but it would not be by studying black, but by learning such things as that 'Black' is not an allowable answer to the question 'What colour is your telephone?'.

Why might we have supposed that black is a colour? Not because it is so like yellow, or even brown, but because telephones and cans of paint come in red, green, black, and so on, and because the word 'black' fits in many of the same slots as 'red', 'green', 'yellow'. If a thing is red it is not green, and not black either, and just as a thing may be yellow and also round, it may be black and also round.

114

If the members of a community did not include black among the colours, would they be wrong? No, they would just be emphasizing a difference that might not interest another community, such as that a film can be either 'in black and white' or 'in colour'. (A community could not be wrong about whether black is a colour, but individuals could be wrong, if in asserting or denying it they were making a claim about how the community uses the word.)

These are all features, actual or possible, of the way these words work. In noting them we are bringing out differences between various words through conducting a close study, like the study we might conduct of various instruments. ('In this one the strings are plucked. In this they are struck. In this they are rubbed. In this there are no strings, but air is blown into chambers of various lengths.')

Part 2

INTRODUCTION

In Part 1 I have been bethinking myself of ways of looking at various kinds of word, given which anyone might agree that yes, that could be a way of seeing that word as an instrument, or yes, it is possible that is the kind of thing Wittgenstein had in mind. In the course of doing this I have frequently stopped to consider what evidence there was that Wittgenstein would agree for example that this word is a quasi-performative, or that one a concealed metaphor; but if in any particular case I found some reason to believe that he would answer that question affirmatively, I did not therefore conclude that seeing the word in the way I had suggested would *be* seeing it as an instrument. A word's being regarded as an instrument *might* be quite a different matter from its being recognized as a quasi-performative, or a concealed metaphor, or what have you.

Operating on the supposition that what is of immediate philosophical value here is not whether words are instruments, or instrument-like, but how they work, I have examined the workings of a number of words, expressions, ways of speaking.

Wittgenstein did not discuss all the words I have investigated but, in the case of words and expressions he did discuss, I have cited such textual evidence as I could as I went along. There is seldom very much of this, and whether a remark of Wittgenstein's counts as evidence is not always very clear. For example my interpretation of *PI* II iv, on the word 'soul', required for its support a somewhat inventive argument. In this and many other cases the most I can claim is that my view combines being consistent with the little that Wittgenstein says, and being of some philosophical interest. But still, *if* I am right in my interpretation of him on the subject of the soul, for

116

example, there is a pattern there that he might quite likely apply to some other words, such as 'mind' or 'conscience'.

While Wittgenstein might disagree with my representations about how this or that word works, and while important things might turn on how the disagreement was resolved, the question at issue would not be whether the word is an instrument, or what it is for a word to be an instrument, but only how that word works.

REVIEW AND ANALYSIS OF TEXTUAL EVIDENCE

If I were to review the most striking pieces of evidence about whether Wittgenstein would agree with my suggestions on the workings of words, as distinct from my theory about what he meant by looking on words as instruments, I would list the following

> 1. Words can be *hard* to say: such for example, as can be used to effect a renunciation, or to confess a weakness. (Words are also deeds.) (*PI* §546)

I am not sure about confessing a weakness, but 'I renounce ...' is clearly a performative speech act. It does something, and it is the disagreeableness of what it may bring about that can make it hard to say. 'Prospective' thinking is required here. The sense in which saying 'I renounce' is a deed is that to say it *is* to renounce, whereas saying the words 'I am walking to work', though also a deed, is not walking to work.

> 2. How did we ever come to use such an expression as 'I believe'? Did we at some time become aware of a phenomenon (of belief)? (*PI* p. 190)

While Wittgenstein did not say so, he almost undoubtedly thought 'not that way anyway'; and that is consistent with a pervasive feature of words having a quasi-performative character: they appear to, but do not, record the occurrence of a phenomenon.

> 3. 'But I do have a real *feeling* of joy.' Yes, when you are glad, you are really glad. And of course joy is not joyful behaviour, nor yet a feeling around the corners of the mouth and the eyes.
>
> 'But "joy" surely designates an inward thing.' No. 'Joy' designates nothing at all. Neither any inward nor any outward thing. (*Z* 487)

If joy designated something, if that were for sure, then if it did not designate something inward it might have to designate behaviour, or *vice versa*. People are driven to behaviourism by not doubting that words like 'joy' designate something. The combination of certainty about that with difficulties about what inward thing it might designate, will seem to leave behaviour as the only alternative. Rejecting the assumption that a word such as 'joy' designates something makes it so far possible to be neither a behaviourist nor a mentalist.

How then does a word such as 'joy' work? For one thing, just as, although one can fake amusement, being amused may just be spontaneously laughing, and there is nothing further called amusement that brings on the laughter, so one can fake delight by saying 'I am delighted', but unfaked delight may be just saying 'I am delighted' spontaneously. Those words are an ejaculation that occurs naturally among language-users, the way a smile of pleasure occurs.

Having said 'I am delighted' one may later say 'I really was (or felt) delighted (joyful, glad)', but there is no difference between 'I really was . . .' and 'I really felt . . .'. Either locution just means that one was not faking it, that one's ejaculation was spontaneous. Hence 'Yes, when you are glad, you really are glad.'

For this to be an effective point against 'But I do have a real *feeling* of joy', it must be implicit (a) that there is no difference between 'I really was . . .' and 'I really felt . . .', and (b) that in saying either of these things one just means that one was not faking it, that it occurred spontaneously. We do not mean that as well as and behind the smile of pleasure or the verbal expression of it there was a feeling. These are notes on the way words such as 'pleasure', 'delight', 'joy' and 'gladness' work. The words do not report or designate anything, but among language-users occur the way smiles and chuckles do.

4. On the subject of concealed metaphors I have cited chiefly *PI* §§373, 423–4, 427, 589; pp. 178, 223; and *Z* 106. the only other passage I might mention is *PI* §112:

> A simile that has been absorbed into the forms of our language produces a false appearance, and this disquiets us.

This mirrors my point that it is because concealed metaphors have come to be among our primary, plain ways of speaking that we tend not to doubt that in using them we are talking about something real, and so are led to ask for example what a mind is.

5. One ought to ask, not what images are or what happens when one imagines anything, but how the word 'imagination' is used. But that does not mean that I want to talk only about words. For the question as to the nature of the imagination is as much a question about the word 'imagination' as my question is. I am only saying that this question is not to be decided – neither for the person who does the imagining, nor for anyone else - by pointing; nor yet by a description of any process. The first question also asks for a word to be explained, but it makes us expect the wrong kind of answer. (*PI* §370; see also §§120, 314, 316, 327, 383.)

Someone might say 'In order to investigate imagining, let's see what happens when we imagine. For my part, I have images. they tend to be less vivid and firm than the things I see, that's clear; but I find it puzzling that it seems impossible to say how large they are or how far away. I can imagine a building 50 metres tall, but I do not suppose my image is that size, and I don't know how to tell what size it actually is. I don't know whether it is larger than the image I had last week of a small cottage. I can imagine a solitary tree on the far side of a large field. The tree may be 400 metres away, but I don't know how far away the image of it is, or indeed from what it is some distance away. I don't know whether to say it is like looking at a picture of such a distant tree. The picture is perhaps 2 metres from my eyes. Is the image similarly some distance from something? I can imagine a tree while looking at a lampshade, and I don't know whether to say that the image is superimposed on the lampshade, or in what manner I manage to have these experiences simultaneously . . .'

Here we would have some supposed findings and some supposed good questions about imagining, the latter seeming to call for closer examination of the phenomena, or awaiting as yet unthought-of techniques of investigation.

To this Wittgenstein might respond 'But how do you know whether you are investigating the right phenomena, or indeed whether there is a phenomenon here to be investigated?' (Cf. *PI* p. 231).

If no likeness of what a person was imagining were appearing before her mind, would it follow that she was not imagining anything? Can one not imagine things of which no likenesses are possible, such as that this person who is laughing is in pain (*PI* §393)?

These need not be conceived as rhetorical questions. The point is that they are to be answered, not by studying the supposed phenomenon of imagining, but by noting how the word 'imagine' is used. The other person's questions can be seen as concealed forms of questions about the use of this word. The question how far away the image is, for example, could be put: 'While "imagine" is used correctly in "I am imagining a solitary tree on the far side of a large field", and also in "How far away do you imagine the tree to be?", is it in order to ask how far away the image of the tree is?' Wittgenstein would say that this is a question, not for close study of the image (if any), but of whether we say 'How far away is your image?', whether those words have a part in the language-game. And the fact that the question stumps us is itself one of the indications that it is not a move in the language-game.

'Memory-*experiences*', Wittgenstein says (*PI* p. 231), 'are *accompaniments* of remembering'; and he might similarly say that the having of images may be an accompaniment of imagining. By this I would take him to mean that he need not deny in any particular case that someone has these experiences, what he questions is whether having them *is* remembering or imagining. If someone says 'There is always an image before my mind when I imagine', Wittgenstein might suggest that this itself indicates that the images accompany, and are not, the imagining. He might add that if one always felt a tickle in the elbow when imagining, that would be no reason for saying that the tickle was the imagining (Cf. *PI* §646).

6. Why don't I call cookery rules arbitrary, and why am I tempted to call the rules of grammar arbitrary? Because 'cookery' is defined by its end, whereas 'speaking' is not. That is why the use of language is in a certain sense autonomous, as cooking and washing are not. You cook badly if you are guided in your cooking by rules other than the right ones; but if you follow other rules than those of chess you are *playing another game*; and if you follow grammatical rules other than such-and-such ones, that does not mean that you say something wrong, no, you are speaking of something else.(*Z* 320)

Here I would have preferred to say that cookery rules are 'determined', rather than 'defined' by their end. They are rules that have been found to yield meals that are tasty and nourishing; but the rules of grammar have not been worked out with a view to dividing reality at its joints, or to producing desired states of mind in people who read or hear what we say, or anything else. Certainly given the rules of grammar we have, a person who violates them will not be understood. Having standard ways of speaking is necessary to our understanding one another; but the specific rules for the use of any word have not been contrived to produce an end, and linguistic standardization requires only that there be rules, does not require that they be of the form that the existing rules have. In this sense language is autonomous (and here I think Wittgenstein's shift from the word 'arbitrary' to the word 'autonomous' was judicious); but I suppose the reason he said he was *tempted* to call the rules of grammar arbitrary, and that the use of language is *in a certain sense* autonomous, is that the design of the language, as distinct from the design of the assertions we make, is not dependent on the nature of the things we talk about, but is still not independent of *everything*.

Wittgenstein suggests in various places (*Z* 355, 357, 364, 366, 378, 388; *PI* §§560, 570, p. 225) that *our* nature has a lot to do with the form of language. By this he may mean that the fact that we are interested in this difference, but not in that, the fact that we can learn one system, but not another, the fact that among systems we can learn, one will be tiresome to use, another not, may often be the reasons why we have concepts that work the way ours do, but the reasons will not have to do with what they are concepts *of*. Indeed concepts prescribe what they are concepts of, rather than objects prescribing the nature of their concepts.

While I have not made a special point of it in discussing various words, the 'autonomy' of language ('in a certain sense') has characterized the accounts I have given of their workings. It is not the nature of beliefs that requires me to say he believes, rather than knows, something if I myself have doubts about whether it is true; it is not the nature of thought that makes it inept to say I have thought about your offer if I have not decided whether to accept it, have no counter-offer to suggest, can indicate no turns of events given which I would accept, and so on.

I have been listing some of the most striking pieces of textual evidence for my accounts of the various ways in which some words work. The question of the textual evidence for the supposition that to look on words as instruments is to think of them as having such 'ways of working' is more difficult, and an area in which I am in greater danger of being shown to be wrong. I have argued that if Wittgenstein disagreed about how this or that word works, that would not show that the invitation to see words as instruments is not an invitation to investigate how they 'work', and hence my thesis is not in danger of being shown to be wrong in that way, although of course, if he meant the invitation some other way, it would follow that whether or not he would agree with my notes on the workings of various words, they could anyway not be represented as his way of seeing words as instruments.

In short two kinds of exegetical question arise here: (i) would Wittgenstein agree with what I have said about this or that word or expression? and (ii) were he to agree, would he agree further that so showing *is* showing how such a word or expression could be regarded as an instrument?

We can now turn to the second of these questions. How strong a claim I can make to be right about whether to see various words in the ways I have depicted them *is* to see them as instruments?

In the passages in *Philosophical Investigations* where anything is called an instrument, we find neither explicit elucidations of what that is supposed to mean, nor examples that might be intended to show how we might go about looking on a word as an instrument.

In places such as *PI* p. 59, Wittgenstein suggests that although one may have been in pain since yesterday, and have understood a word since yesterday, the understanding, unlike the pain, either can't have been continuous or would not be called discontinuous on the ground that something that had been happening had let up for a time. This could be called a comparison of some of the workings of the words 'pain' and 'understanding', and might therefore be a way of seeing these words as instruments but, since it is not marked as an example of that, it is no help in deciding what Wittgenstein may have meant.

If some points like those on p. 59, although not marked as a way of seeing words as instruments, followed on the heels of a suggestion that words are instruments, or were immediately followed by such a remark, they might be used as evidence; but there are no examples that, either by their location or by being marked as cases in point, help us to decide the interpretive question.

However there may be other indications. If Wittgenstein has been discussing a problem and, without clearly resolving it, introduces the idea that words are instruments as if it would help in disposing of the difficulty, then the fact that we can make headway with that problem using one supposition about what it might be for a word to be an instrument, but not or not so well on the basis of other suppositions, may count as evidence; or if he follows an invitation to see words as instruments with remarks that make better sense on one interpretation than on others, that too may count as evidence. These are the main kinds of consideration to which I will appeal in the following review of the key passages.

In reviewing these, I propose to ignore the differences between the German '*Instrument*', '*Mittel*', '*Werkzeug*'and '*Vorrichtung*', unless the context makes it clear that, of these four, only the word actually used would serve to make Wittgenstein's point.

Sometimes when one or other of these words appears it is obvious that Wittgenstein had no intention of contributing anything to the view that words can be regarded as instruments or tools or what have you. For example *PI* §41, where he is talking about a tool that is called 'N', is not relevant because he is not saying that the *word* 'N' is a tool, and he could equally have used building blocks or items of furniture as examples.

The relevant passages are:

> 1. What about the colour samples A shews to B: are they part of the *language*? Well, it is as you please. They do not belong among the words; yet when I say to someone 'Pronounce the word "the"', you will count the second 'the' as part of the sentence. Yet it has a role just like that of a colour sample in language-game (8); that is, it is a sample of what the other is meant to say. It is most natural, and causes least confusion, to reckon the samples among the instruments [*Werkzeugen*] of the language. (*PI* §16)

Here I do not know whether to suppose that Wittgenstein wants to say that there is language proper, consisting of words, and then there are tools of language, the latter not being words, but still being parts of a system of communication. That would be a basis for declining (as he does here) to give a flat 'yes' or 'no' answer to the question whether the colour samples are part of the language, and would be in line with his saying, as he does, 'Well, it is as you please'; but on the other hand, mindful of the fact that he later calls words too instruments, we might suppose him to be thinking that language consists of instruments, some of which are words, and others samples (of colour, sound, shape, and so on), and that all these instruments are equally parts of language. Without pronouncing on that question, (after all it is 'as you please', and it is only a matter of what is most natural) I shall just note that, in saying that the second 'the' has a role just like that of a colour sample in language-game (8), Wittgenstein is saying something about how they both work: they function as guides, in one case in making a sound, and in others in choosing building materials or apples, and so on. It is not perfectly clear though whether in calling them instruments he is adverting to this manner of functioning.

2. In *PI* §50 Wittgenstein imagines samples of colour kept hermetically sealed in Paris to define colour words. He says

> This sample [of sepia] is an instrument (*Instrument*) of the language used in ascriptions of colour. In this language-game it is not something that is represented but is a means [*Mittel*] of representation. . . . It is a paradigm in our language-game, something with which comparison is made.

Here it might look as if to be an instrument is to be a paradigm, something with which comparison is made; but there is no reason for preferring that reading to one in which being a paradigm is merely one of the ways of being an instrument: some linguistic instruments work that way, others in other ways. The latter reading is obviously more in line with my interpretive hypothesis, and there is a strong reason for preferring it: words too are supposed to be instruments but, while the second 'the' in 'Pronounce the word "the"' works as a paradigm, with which comparison is made, that is a very special case, and normally words are not paradigms. 'Bring a large slab' does not mean 'Among things like *the word* "slab", bring one that is like *the word* "large"'

One can record observations about how paradigms work, and Wittgenstein did some of this in this section. He said (*PI*

§50) 'There is *one* thing of which one can say neither that it is one metre long, nor that it is not one metre long, and that is the standard metre in Paris. – But this of course is not to ascribe any extraordinary property to it, but only to mark its peculiar role in the language-game of measuring with a metre rule.' (He makes a similar point about the imagined paradigm of sepia.)

Elsewhere (*RC* 131) he notes a difference between 'That book is a darker colour than this', and 'That colour is darker than this.' The latter gives a paradigm of what 'darker' means in colour contexts, while the former applies an established paradigm to a pair of objects.

These are some of the ways paradigms work. There is no strong indication that in calling them instruments Wittgenstein was inviting us to think about how they work, but since in close proximity he called them instruments and displayed some of their workings, that hypothesis is at least plausible – and more plausible than the only other reading likely to emerge from this passage, according to which to call anything an instrument is to say it is a paradigm.

3. A similar point can be taken from *PI* §53. Wittgenstein describes a table used in teaching colour language and appealed to in disputed cases, a table in which various 'signs' are connected with various colour samples. He says 'We can also imagine such a table's being a tool [*Werkzeug*] in the use of the language. Describing a complex [such as that in *PI* §48] is then done like this: the person who describes the complex has a table with him and looks up each element of the complex in it, and passes to the sign (and the one who is given the description may also use the table to translate it into a picture of coloured squares).' Here he calls the table a tool, and then describes how it works.

4. In *PI* §54 Wittgenstein says

Let us recall the kinds of case where a game is played according to a definite rule . . . The rule may be an aid in teaching the game. The learner is told it and given practice in applying it. – Or it is an instrument [*Werkzeug*] of the game itself. – Or a rule is employed neither in the teaching nor in the game itself; nor is it set down in a list of rules. But we say it is played according to such-and-such rules because an observer can read these rules off from the practice of the game. . . .

Here it is obscure what might be meant by a rule being an

instrument of the game itself, as distinct from the other two suggested senses in which there may be rules of a game. All I can suggest is that he is talking about tactical rules such as the rule in chess that in the first several moves one should get as many pieces into play as possible; but I have not found a way in which this sheds any light on what he means by instruments.

> 5. . . . When we forget which colour this is the name of, it loses its meaning for us, that is we are no longer able to play a particular language-game with it. And the situation then is comparable with that in which we have lost a paradigm which was an instrument [*Mittel*] of our language.

This passage is so like §50 in the way it connects instruments and paradigms that it would seem to yield nothing new.

> 6. What we call 'descriptions' are instruments [*Instruments*] for particular uses. Think of a machine-drawing, a cross-section, an elevation with measurements, which an engineer has before him. Thinking of a description as a word-picture of the facts has something misleading about it: one tends to think only of such pictures as hang on our walls: which seem simply to portray how a thing looks, what it is like. (These pictures are as it were idle.)
> (*PI* §291)

In the section preceding this, Wittgenstein said 'Perhaps the word "describe" tricks us here. I say "I describe my state of mind" and "I describe my room". You need to call to mind the differences between the language-games.' What are these differences? He does not say, but two examples we have seen might be acceptable to him. As an answer to the question 'How serious are you about this?', a question about my state of mind, I may say 'With some encouragement from you I would do it.' that describes my state of mind, but not in the way 'There is a large window facing east, framed prints on the walls and a bookcase near the door' describes my room. The description of my state of mind is a kind of offer, and it is not 'as it were idle'.

Again if I say I am very depressed, or I am sorry I did it, I can be seen as doing something, moping in one case, apologizing in another. These words are again not 'as it were idle', but we can say they describe my state of mind; and it is uncommonly hard to suggest what description of these states of mind one might construct that would compare with a description of my room. If I say 'I keep saying to myself "Oh, why can't things go better for me?!", and feeling as if I were about to cry', that is indeed more like a description of my room, but still it will come across as a way of saying I am depressed only if in reporting these events I am treating them as genuine manifestations of depression. The genuineness of these thoughts and feelings is not an ascertainable fact about them, a report of which if believed would show them to be genuine. It is my mentioning them in enlarging on how depressed I have been that shows them to have been manifestations of depression, rather than perhaps a puzzling phenomenon that occurred after taking some drug, and left me disinclined to say I was depressed.

These examples, arising out of the preceding section, may illustrate one way in which something may be a description without being a word-picture of the facts. I think we should take it that the examples of machine-drawings, cross-sections and elevations with measurements in *PI* §291 bring out a second and different way. Take a cross-section. 'This is what you would see if you could cut it through at this point (or at this angle through this point).' A cross-section, say of the hull of a yacht, however accurate it may be, is not a picture of the hull, and will not generally render anything that its author or anyone else has seen; but if one understands the conventions governing such drawings, the cross-section is a useful device for explaining the hull contours. It is a device that works in a somewhat complicated way that one must learn, and a way different from that in which an elevation with measurements works. The way in which it is not 'as it were idle' is that it does not passively reflect what one would see with the naked eye or in a photograph, but employs an inventive system of representation to bring out facts about the hull contours.

Machine-drawings, cross-sections and elevations are presumably employed here as an explanatory analogy, to bring out something about less formalized descriptions. An example might be this: in giving testimony in court about an accident scene, one might well mention that it was foggy, but not that it was overcast; that the traffic was heavy, but not what makes or colours the vehicles were; that one of the drivers was making a left turn, but not why he wanted to make it, and so on. What we would want to know about the scene is described by the system for determining legal liability. Someone who was not interested in this, but thought the scene had aesthetic appeal and might make a good subject for a painting, might mention the long shadows in the afternoon light, the colour contrasts, the anxious faces of the bystanders. Different interests prescribe different descriptions, and the artist's impression of the scene would likely be found irrelevant if presented in a courtroom while a police officer's description would not likely be of use in the studio.

We have one kind of descriptive instrument in the case of states of mind, and quite a different kind, working in an entirely different way, in the case of cross-sections and so on. The latter cases bear more of a resemblance to different kinds of descriptions of accident scenes, the chief point of resemblance being that the description is determined more by the purposes of the person describing than by the nature of the object described.

None of these descriptions is 'as it were idle'. They do not simply reflect what is there, but (in different ways) approach what is there with a system of some complexity, or with a set of interests that determines what will form part of the description.

> 7. But a machine surely cannot think! – Is that an empirical statement? No. We only say of a human being and what is like one that it thinks. We also say it of dolls and no doubt of spirits too. Look on the word 'to think' as a tool [*Instrument*]. (*PI* §360)

There is no specific help provided here on how we might go about looking on the verb 'to think' as an instrument. However there may be a clue in the fourth sentence of the section. If it is said only of human beings and what is like them that they think then, given that machines are too unlike human beings, the claim is, not that machines do not think, but that *we do not say* that they think.

But does no one say that machines think? 'We do not say that machines think' could mean either that nobody says 'Machines think', an empirical proposition that is undoubtedly false, or that whereas we say both 'She thought about it' and 'She did it without thinking', we do not say either 'The calculator thought about whether to do the multiplication' or 'Without thinking, it put "652" as the product of 25 multiplied by 25', nor do we reproach a machine with the words 'No, no.

You weren't thinking what you were doing!'

These latter are to be read, not as empirical propositions, but as grammatical remarks: we *make no sense* of the idea of reproaching a machine with not thinking.

Since we do not say 'People think' (when did you ever hear that said?), but do say for example 'He tried to think of her name', and do not say 'Without thinking, the machine . . .', it is likely that Wittgenstein was making the grammatical rather than the empirical point; and this is confirmed by the bafflement he expresses in *PI* §361 at the idea of attributing thought to a chair. He may be suggesting that, just as we lose our bearings when a chair is said to be thinking, so we can make no sense of the idea of reproaching a machine with not thinking what it is doing, or encouraging it to try again more attentively.

Similarly, if a machine produced the words 'I have thought about your problem', we would not suppose it was broaching a discussion, or offering its help. We might program a computer to show these words at the point at which it was ready to deliver a solution, and set it to withhold the answer until we typed in the words 'Well, what's the solution?', but this would be for amusement only, and would be no different from fixing it to show the word 'Ready' until we typed in the word 'Go'. Similarly if a word processor showed the word 'thinking' during the interval when it was finding all the appearances of a certain word in a file, it might equally (or better) say 'Wait', and we would not in the former case suppose it was thinking because after all it said so, and would have no reason to deceive us.

Hence I would suggest Wittgenstein is trying to divert us from a dumb way of thinking about whether machines think, in which we regard the question as one of whether a distinctive, hard to describe, conscious process could occur in a calculator or a computer – if not in presently known ones, perhaps in imaginable future models. We may have wondered: if this process occurs in human brains, why might there not be an artifact, in principle like a brain, in which it also occurred? Of course we would recognize that, even if it were occurring, it would be awfully hard to tell, since if a machine said it was thinking we would not know whether to believe it, and we could not conclude it had been thinking just because it had done a calculation, because we know that machines calculate, and we are still not sure whether they think.

Wittgenstein may have wanted to replace this way of regarding the question with one in which the issue was one of whether a machine could occupy the social place, so to speak, of a person here: whether a machine could be reproached with not thinking when it made a mistake, whether it could be encouraged to think carefully, whether it could broach a discussion of a problem or offer help with it, or be uncertain whether to say it had been thinking because what had been occurring was rather too undisciplined to be honoured with that description.

If the intent of the encouragement to look on the verb 'to think' as an instrument was in this way to get us to reflect on the way the word works in human interactions, we may still not be able to derive from these reflections an answer to the question whether it is conceivable that a machine might think. This would now be a question, not of whether there might ever be a machine in which a certain distinctive conscious process occurred, but of whether there might be one that could occupy what I have called the 'social place' of a person in ways like those illustrated. The latter question might still call for an answer, but it is doubtful whether, as philosophers, we should have a stake in answers to such questions, rather than in understanding the kind of questions they are. It would be clear enough that no presently existing machine occupies the place in which a person is cast by our uses of the word 'think', but someone might say she could imagine a machine enough like a person that these encouragements, reproaches, broachings, offers and doubts would seem natural enough. That need not worry Wittgenstein. He said 'We only say of a human being and what is like one that it thinks', and such a machine *might* be enough like a human being.

It would still not be clear whether seeing the word as an instrument would be a matter of considering what it is used *for* (for example, reproaching, encouraging), or whether it would be a matter of considering what it is about it that enables it to do these things. The two features are closely related; but it is at least possible, and perhaps likely, that it is the latter that should be emphasized, since as I argued in the section on concealed metaphors, the reproach 'You weren't thinking!' itself works by trading on the idea of an imaginary auxiliary activity. We seem to be saying there was something, the doing of which was omitted; but this is only a way of saying that you made a mistake that you knew better than to make. We would not have made a clean break with the conception of thinking as a characteristic conscious process unless we took some such view as this on how the word works.

The exegetical argument here is that since Wittgenstein enjoined looking on the word 'think' as an instrument in the context of a discussion of whether machines think, and since on my interpretation of what it is to look on a word as an instrument a vigorous point about whether machines think emerges, there is that much reason for thinking the interpretation sound. The argument would be stronger if it included a claim that *only* on this interpretation does such a dividend accrue; but exegetical arguments can hardly hope to be that strong.

8. In *PI* §421, having suggested that it might seem paradoxical that we should mix physical states and states of consciousness up together in a single report, such as 'He suffered great torments and tossed about restlessly', Wittgenstein suggests that a sentence such as 'These three struts give the building stability' does not worry us, although three and stability are not tangible, and then says 'Look at the sentence as an instrument, and its sense as its employment.'

It is initially quite mystifying how this last comes out as a helpful suggestion in the context, and Wittgenstein does not enlarge on it, so again an effort of invention will be required; but the following may be found plausible.

It may be important to decide first whether he is saying that it is all right to mix tangibles and intangibles together, as is shown in the example of the tree struts giving the building stability; or whether his point is rather that three and stability are not intangibles, and therefore there is no mixing of the tangible and the intangible here, and neither is there such mixing in the case of the torments and the tossing.

The latter reading seems more likely to be Wittgenstein's view. Just as he does not make sense of 'Thinking is not an incorporeal process' (*PI* §339), we may suppose he would make no sense of 'Suffering torment is not an intangible process.' It is indeed not tangible, but it no more follows from this that it is intangible, than it follows from the fact that thought is not coloured, that it is colourless (like clean air). To say that thought is not coloured is to say that colour words, including 'colourless', do not apply to it; and 'Stability is not tangible' is the same kind of remark.

Since 'intangible' is a problem word like 'incorporeal', and it is not very clear how it is to be marshalled, it may be better if we change the question to one of whether stability has a shape, or a size, the way a slab or a pillar may. Clearly stability can be neither round, square, nor any other shape, and neither large, small or any other size; but only if it were nevertheless some kind of object would this show it to be an occult object. However the stability of a building is not one of its parts, the way a joist or a stringer is.

Similarly perhaps Wittgenstein means to suggest that, while restless tossing may be a state of a tangible object, torment is not a state of an intangible one. If we say torment is a state of consciousness, it is likely that Wittgenstein would say no, it is a state of a person (cf. *PI* §573); but even if he allowed that it is a state of consciousness, he would reject the argument that it is therefore a state of something intangible. It might be argued that since consciousness is neither round, square nor any other shape, neither large, small nor any other size, neither heavy, light nor any other weight, and so on, it is intangible. The premises here are true, but they would show consciousness to be intangible (insubstantial, immaterial) only if it were for all that an *object*. An object having no size, shape or weight (no size whatever, that is, not just a minuscule size) is certainly not a material object; but only if it is at any rate an object is it therefore an immaterial object. Similarly if consciousness is no kind of object, its lack of colour, size, shape and weight will not show it to be an immaterial object.

To decide whether consciousness is an object, Wittgenstein can be read here as suggesting that we consider on what occasions we say for example 'I am conscious.' (The sentence's sense is its employment.) He had raised this question four sections earlier (§417), and (oddly enough) had given an answer in §416: 'I tell someone who believes I am in a faint "I am conscious again".'

This remark does not itself take us very far. We *could* regard these words as reporting the return of something, but as we saw in the discussion of consciousness in Part 1, there is a difficulty here, in that consciousness is not conceived as an object like any other, of the comings and goings of which a conscious person might be a spectator. 'I am conscious' does have the ring of 'I am in pain', but it is not used the same way. One can say 'I am no longer in pain', but not 'I am no longer conscious.' The latter does not record the departure of something that could be noticed alongside of pains and itches; and while we can disbelieve someone who says she is in pain, we can hardly disbelieve the person who says he is conscious. (*Z* 401–2)

I suggested that 'I am conscious' is an instrument in that it works this way: it is a way of saying something and thereby showing that one is conscious, without saying anything in particular. Saying one's head aches or asking for some water would serve just as well, but if one has nothing in particular like that to say, one might just say 'I am speaking', or 'attend to the fact that I am saying something', either of which would serve the same purpose as 'I am conscious.'

Here I have been looking on the sentence 'I am conscious' as an instrument by remembering how it is employed. What we found is that, although consciousness (or being conscious) does not have the properties of a material thing, it is not therefore an immaterial thing. We are not talking about something that might have properties, but saying 'I shall hear if I am not deaf, see if I am not blind, feel if I am not paralysed, and so on.'

> 9. To invent a language could mean to invent an instrument [*Vorrichtung*] for a particular purpose on the basis of the laws of nature (or consistently with them); but it also has the other sense, analogous to that in which we speak of the invention of a game. Here I am stating something about the grammar of the word 'language', by connecting it with the grammar of the word 'invent' (*PI* §492).

As previously noted (p. 7), there is no need here to suppose that, in the 'other' sense of inventing a language, language is not an instrument, just that it is a different kind of instrument. Whereas it is imaginable that there should be a language based on a number of discoveries such as that people approach when they hear the sound 'come' and move off when they hear the sound 'go', a language that worked through its words affecting people in such ways, Wittgenstein no doubt thought that the business of inventing a language would not involve such discoveries, but would be like inventing a game, where the endeavour will be successful if it yields something that will suit human beings.

(I do not know why he said he was saying something about the grammars of the words 'language' and 'invent', rather than just that he was saying what kind of business inventing a language would be. This might be a fruitful question.)

Whether or not it is a grammatical point, we are left with the suggestion that a language is not based on discoveries, but is an invention that, like a game, will be successful if it suits human beings. This is of a piece with what emerged from *Z* 320 (pp. 120-1 above) about the sense in which language is 'autonomous', and in that sense the ways of working that were delineated in Part 1 all cast language as being 'autonomous'.

It may be significant also that in §492 'instrument' is the translation of the German '*Vorrichtung*', which means 'mechanism' or 'device', and mechanisms and devices, more than hammers and scalpels, are things the workings of which may be investigated.

(I presume that Wittgenstein is talking here about inventing *a* language, not about inventing language, that is, something that might have occurred in the pre-history of the human race. Very different conclusions might emerge from the latter supposition, but Wittgenstein probably does not think that inventing language is possible (see for example *PI* §§25, 120). Before there came to be any languages, no one could say 'I have an idea, chaps. Let's agree on a set of noises . . .'.

10. The final passage in the *Investigations* where something linguistic is represented as an instrument is §569, in which we read 'Language is an instrument. Its concepts are instruments.' Wittgenstein goes on to discuss whether, that being the case, it will make a difference which concepts we employ. He considers whether it might be just a matter of convenience, as it is with the question whether to do physics in feet and inches or metres and centimetres, and against this says that it would not be just a matter of convenience if a system of measurement demanded more time and trouble than it was possible to give it. Some preliminary points about this passage:

(i) Whereas 'Look on the word "to think" as an instrument' would be consistent with the view that some words are instruments, or are instrument-like, and others not, the pronouncement here is very sweeping, and seems to make it necessary to find a sense in which *every* word is an instrument.

(ii) I know of no place where it becomes quite clear what Wittgenstein means by a concept, but in *PI*§208 he says 'I shall explain these words to someone who, say, only speaks French by means of the corresponding French words. But if a person has not yet got the *concepts*, I shall teach him how to use the words by means of *examples* and by practice.' It seems fair to conclude from this that a concept is a word token that has an established use. The person who knows how to use the corresponding French words 'has the concept', while the person who can use neither the English word nor the corresponding word in any other language does not. What the former has and the latter lacks is the ability to use the word in the established way.

(I take it that generally when Wittgenstein says something about 'the word so and so', he does not mean the word token, but the token as used in an established way, or the concept.)

(iii) It is not clear whether Wittgenstein would accept as an alternative to 'Language is an instrument. Its concepts are instruments', 'Both language and its concepts are instruments', or whether he would prefer 'Language is an instrument, *that is to say* its concepts are instruments.' If he would prefer the latter, he wrote ineptly, since it would clearly be preferable in that case to say, not 'Language is an instrument', but 'Language is comprised of instruments'; but not on every conception of an instrument will it be easy to see how language itself might be an instrument.

When language is viewed as a system, however, or a set of systems, it will be an instrument in the sense that it has a complicated way of working that can be investigated. We can find out for example, just from studying the system, that if something is red it is not yellow or blue or. . ., but may be scarlet, whereas if it is not red it is not scarlet either; and that if it is any colour it must have some shape and size, but need not be round or rectangular or 96 centimetres in length. We can discover similarly that a man can be 2 metres tall, but not 2 metres long, and that a sphere can be neither 2 metres long nor 2 metres tall. These are notes on the way the English language works, and the fact that they thus provide a sense in which language itself might be called an instrument counts as some evidence for my interpretive thesis.

(iv) The fact that Wittgenstein takes what he says here to suggest that it can make no great difference which concepts we employ may limit what he can mean by saying that language and its concepts are instruments, if its making no great difference would appear to follow on some interpretations and not on others. If there were a task to be performed using a concept (if that makes sense), and the concept was artfully designed in such a way as to perform that function, the way a scalpel is designed to make incisions, it would clearly make a considerable difference what concept (instrument) we employed; whereas, if concepts were conceived on the model of a kind of signal, say a signal that dinner was ready, or that the crocuses were blooming, it might make no great difference, might be only a matter of convenience, whether we rang a gong, raised a flag or flashed lights. Especially since in §492 Wittgenstein rejected a supposition quite like the former, the latter seems so far more likely.

That reading is rendered doubtful however partly by the fact that in the third sentence Wittgenstein appears to be saying only that it will *seem* to make no great difference which concepts we employ, and partly by the fact that in the final sentence of the section he appears to reject the idea that it is just a matter of convenience. However, the fact that on a given reading it should even *seem* to make no great difference may be important, if it does not even seem that way on other readings.

(v) Wittgenstein's point in the final sentence does not seem to me well crafted but, whether or not the reason he gives is a good one, he does reject the idea that what concepts we have is merely a matter of convenience. The fact that using some concepts would demand more time and trouble than it is possible to give them only makes them too inconvenient altogether, and leaves it possible that all the concepts we do use survive because they are convenient; leaves it possible that we have this one, not that, because the former is more convenient.

The convenience theory goes with the idea of a separation between a job to be done and the instrument devised for doing it. Since Wittgenstein opposes the convenience theory, he may oppose the idea of this separation. There are at least two understandings of the nature of a concept, given which this separation would collapse or disappear: (a) if the idea of the job to be done were built into the concept, and (b) if the job came into being with the concept.

(a) If we wanted a signal that dinner was ready and said 'Let it be ringing this bell three times', the job to be done would thereby be built into the signal. Ringing the bell thrice would thereafter be saying that dinner was ready. It would do this job neither efficiently nor inefficiently, unlike the way a rasp may be a more efficient device for grinding metal than a stone. It would just do it. Ringing a bell might be more convenient or less convenient than flashing lights, but ringing the bell or flashing the lights (whichever we had settled on) would *be* doing the job.

A more interesting question than that of convenience (and so possibly a question Wittgenstein, in rejecting convenience, preferred) is that of why we want the job done at all. Which signal to have may be a matter of convenience, but whether to have one at all is a matter of what we care about, or of how we want to live.

(b) In one of the discussions of believing in Part 1, I suggested that we say 'He believes that P', rather than 'He knows that P', when the speaker, not the believer, has doubts about whether P is true. To say he knows that P is to say that P is true and that he is apprized of this, whereas to say he believes that P is to say that he says or holds that P, but I do not care to say what I think about whether P is true. (This is of course not true if we say 'He believes it but 'I know it', but I suggested that 'emphatic' uses of 'believe' and 'know' work differently.)

Did we want a short way of saying that P is true and he is apprized of this, or that he holds that P, but I do not care to say whether it is true – and contrive 'He knows that P' and 'He believes that P' as convenient ways of saying these things? Or might we have already had certain uses of 'know' and 'believe', and found that given them we could not say 'He knows that P' unless we would ourselves say that P is true, and so have fallen into these ways of using 'know' and 'believe'? I do not wish to make any historical claim about this. My point is that the latter supposition is entirely possible, and that if so the idea of jointly expressing one's own and another person's estimation of the truth of a proposition might have come into being, not because we perceived a need to do this and devised way of doing it, but because part of the previously established use of 'know' and 'believe' seemed to require it. A way of speaking would thereby be generated. It would be neither a convenient nor an inconvenient way of doing the job it does, it would just do it; but whether we saw fit to make use of the mechanism thereby provided would be a question like the question why one game is widely played and another not. Chess is not a convenient way of doing something that could be done in other ways, but a game that interests (some) people; and similarly these ways of using 'believe' and 'know' are in use, not because they provide a convenient way of doing the jobs they do, but because for example 'He says *P*, but I'm not so sure' is something we sometimes want to say.

My question was, on what understanding of the assertion that language and its concepts are instruments would it appear to follow that it did not matter greatly which concepts we employed, while further reflection would show that this was not just a matter of convenience? The answer I have suggested is that, if there were jobs to be done, and concepts were artfully devised to do them, it would make a considerable difference what concepts we contrived, whereas, if the job to be done were thought of as something conventionally attached to a word, it would certainly not matter to what word the job was attached. There is this much reason for supposing the latter to be Wittgenstein's view; and that supposition is confirmed by the fact that further reflection shows that, while it may not matter what word token we employ, nevertheless, since the *concept* is different if the job is different, what *concept* we employ will matter greatly, and will not be a matter of convenience. There will be no difference between the concept and the job such as would make it possible for the concept to be a convenient or an inconvenient device for doing the job, but only a question of whether the job is one we want done. Since this is how things appear on my analyses of various concepts (I gave as examples only some aspects of the use of 'know' and 'believe', but the point could be shown to apply quite generally), this reading of §569 shows it so far to support my thesis.

On the supposition that a pregnant passage, like the first two sentences of §569, may often sum up, in however cryptic a way, the point of the discussion that precedes it, I would like now to review some of Wittgenstein's deliberations, beginning at §547, about whether and why we would say, in some problem cases, that a word has more than one meaning. Some examples are 'is' in 'The snow is white' and in 'Twice two is four', 'one' in 'The rod is one yard long' and in 'Here is one soldier', and in an imaginary language, 'X' and 'Y', which when used singly are like our 'not', but doubling 'X' cancels the negation, while doubling 'Y' reinforces it.

In some of these cases Wittgenstein seems to be in no doubt that the word does have a different meaning in the contrasted sentences, and one of the tests he uses is whether any word that can be substituted for the problem word in one of the sentences can replace it in the other. Instead of 'Twice two is four' we can say 'Twice two equals four', but we cannot replace 'is' with 'equals in 'The rose is red' (§558). He makes this point in rejecting an imagined contention that there is only one set of rules governing the word 'is', which allow its use in both the sentences, and that therefore the word has only one meaning. (He had *accepted* a similar claim about the word 'understand' in §532).

He discusses whether the use of a word is determined by the nature of the phenomenon to which we refer in using it, whether for example 'to negate' is the name of an action, and the word 'not' in a sentence tells us to perform this action of negating, and whether it is because of the nature of this action that a double negative is an affirmative. Against this he makes three points.

(1) We can't say what this action is, and would have to say something fishy, such as that it is an action we all know of and only have to be reminded of (§549)

(2) We can't say that the rules for the use of 'not' (such as that a double negative is an affirmative) accord with its meaning (or can't raise the question whether the rules might inaccurately reflect its meaning) because the rules give the word its meaning and if we were to change the rules it would have another meaning, or none (cf. *Z* 320; *PI* note (b) p. 147; p. 231).

(3) He suggests that we might give three different accounts of why doubling 'X' counts as affirming, while doubling 'Y' reinforces the negation: we could say either (a) that 'X' as it were turns the sense through 180°, but that 'Y' is like shaking the head; or (b) that the *words* 'X' and 'Y' have different meanings, since they have different uses, but similar *sentences* in which they appear singly have the same meaning, except that by a caprice of language they have come to have different senses when doubled.

139

I suggest that, in this section, in setting out three answers to the question about the meaning of 'X' and 'Y', Wittgenstein is not supposing that at most one of them is correct, but rather than any one of them would do well enough. I have no conclusive reason for this interpretation, but his saying 'We could give various answers to this', rather than for example 'Should we say (a) or (b) or (c)?' suggests it, as does the somewhat cryptic remark in §560 'The meaning of a word is what is explained by the explanation of the meaning.' This I read, not as resembling the platitude 'The bicycle is what is described by the description of the bicycle', but as resembling 'His proposal is what is described in paragraph seven' (cf. *PI* §367). If I am right about this, there is not a distinct something that is the meaning, the way there is a distinct something that is the bicycle, and hence there is nothing the nature of which could show which of these answers to the question about 'X' and 'Y' is correct. We could have got this conclusion just from the initial description of 'X' and 'Y'. We were told all there was to tell about them in being told that when used singly they are like our 'not', but doubling 'X' cancels the negation, while doubling 'Y' reinforces it (cf. *PI* §10).

In *PI* note (a), p. 147, Wittgenstein says

> 'It looks as if it followed from the nature of negation that a double negative is an affirmative. (And there is something right about this. What? Our nature is connected with both.)

Here it is peculiarly difficult to say *what* two things Wittgenstein has in mind as being connected with our nature, but I am inclined to suggest that they are (i) the disposition to think that it follows from the nature of negation that a double negative is an affirmative, and (ii) the fact that a double negative is an affirmative. I do not understand how the fact that our nature is connected with both would show that there is something right about saying it follows from the nature of negation that a double negative is an affirmative, but I do see how there would be something right about its looking as if it followed, if our nature were connected with this *seeming to follow*.

How is our nature connected with this? Perhaps by our having a general tendency to become confused when we think about the language we use, rather than just using it.

More interesting is the question how our nature might be connected with the fact that in our language a double negative is an affirmative. We might have had it otherwise, and would not have been *wrong* in that event; but perhaps people with a nature different from ours would never entirely master our use of of the double negative because they could not rid their minds of the picture of negating as shaking the head, and thus of further head-shaking as more emphatic negating; whereas perhaps it is our nature just to learn this linguistic twist and think no more about it – not to expect that there will be a rationale.

References to our nature might also explain why we have double negatives at all. Why do we sometimes say it is not the case that *P* is not true, rather than just that *P* is true? The answer might be because we converse and discuss, and when someone has said that *P* is not true, we sometimes want to bring out in our response that what we say is intended to controvert what the other person has said. 'What you said is not true' brings this out, and substituting what *was* said for the words 'what you said', we get '"*P* is not true" is not true'. We might have managed without this linguistic turn. Our having it reflects our nature as beings that discuss and dispute.

What emerges from this is again a picture of concepts as being 'autonomous' in the sense that their nature is not determined by that of the objects (if any) they are concepts of, and they are not in danger of being shown to be incorrect by discoveries about those objects. Concepts are however related to our nature, but still not in such a way that discoveries about or changes in our nature would show them to be incorrect, rather than perhaps infelicitous. The relation here is more like that between games and the people who play them. If I get bored with poker and do not play it any more, I may have discovered that the proposition that I enjoy it is false, but not that the game incorrectly reflects my nature.

Since Wittgenstein's pronouncement that language is an instrument, its concepts are instruments follows on the heels of this picture of the status of language and its concepts, it is fair to suppose that the picture explains part of what is meant by the pronouncement. The thought that concepts are 'autonomous' sits best with the idea that like most instruments they have an internal complexity that may be investigated and that does not reflect the nature of what they are concepts of, even when they are concepts of something, and so we may attribute that thought to Wittgenstein with whatever confidence is warranted by the foregoing somewhat involved argument.

SUMMARY

None of the passages I have reviewed shows at all clearly what Wittgenstein meant in calling words, sentences and so on instruments, and when an effort of invention is required to bring out what might have been meant, it is always possible that a different interpretation might be constructed that would be just as plausible. Perhaps the most that one can show is that a certain interpretation is consistent with, rather than required by, the textual evidence; but while two interpretations may be equally consistent with a given passage, the likelihood of their both being consistent with all the relevant passages decreases with each additional text. A defender of an alternative interpretation would have some work to do to show for example how looking on the verb 'to think' as an instrument in some other sense would enable one to make headway with the question whether machines think, or why it is that, if language and its concepts are instruments, it will look as if it did not matter greatly which concepts we employ, as well as to show why this would be a mistake.

Still, the most I can claim is to have made out a case for my reading and, by putting a contender in the field, to have got serious discussion started, and to have brought out where some of the issues lie.

On the questions that have arisen, I have made assumptions that could certainly be questioned. For example in considering the question in §556 whether 'X' and 'Y' have the same meaning in sentences in which they occur without being repeated, I treated Wittgenstein's three answers as intended to be all equally acceptable, rather than as being candidates between which we would have to choose. My assumption had some consequences, but my justification of it was far from conclusive. However I did raise a question here, the answer to which makes a difference, and the need for answering which might not have been noticed.

Part 3

WHAT ARE THE CONSEQUENCES?

While Wittgenstein did not say so, it is fairly obvious in most of the passages in which he suggests that words and so on are instruments that he thinks it will make an important difference whether one appreciates this; and for my part, if I did not suppose it would be a matter of some philosophical consequence what he meant, I would be reluctant to devote much energy to answering that question. I have often shown in particular contexts what philosophical difference the view I was attributing to him might make; in this part I wish to give a general statement of the differences, and their importance. If the consequences appear to be of a characteristically Wittgensteinian kind, that may itself count as some evidence of the correctness of the interpretation; but, to repeat a point made earlier, it is possible that Wittgenstein would subscribe to many of the points I have made about this or that concept, and to the consequences I draw, although these points are not what he would offer as illustrations of what he means when he recommends thinking of words as instruments.

My interpretive thesis may be summarized briefly as follows: calling words instruments is a way of saying that, like instruments, they work in various ways. Just as we can investigate how an instrument works, we can find out how a given word works. Since the 'workings' of a word are not before us when we hear it or see it on the page, we do not come naturally to appreciate that words *have* workings, still less what they are from case to case; and since words seem to differ only in such obvious ways as in their sounds or spellings, and in whether they are nouns, verbs, adjectives, . . . we take it that a question that regularly and properly arises about one word (like 'What is waltzing?') will of course arise about an apparently similar word ('What is thinking?'). Pursuing such questions about words that are in fact dissimilar in their workings is one of the ways we get into philosophical difficulties; and we can avoid these difficulties, not by improving our ways of answering the questions, but by tracking down differences in the ways the words that puzzle us work, thereby often discovering that the question we have been pressing does not properly arise, and does not require an answer.

I have distinguished a number of characteristic kinds of way in which words may work, and these may provide some guidance in what to look for in shifting for oneself in new cases; but there may be both workings that are not of any of these types, and important differences between words that are of a given type, and hence in this work there is no substitute for ferreting out the fine detail. (This is particularly clear in the case of what I called 'variant models'.)

When cast in the way I have just done, the thought that words are instruments may appear to add nothing that might not have been known in understanding such conceptions of Wittgenstein's as those of grammatical illusions, surface and depth grammar, and philosophy as the art of dissolving rather than solving problems; but the idea that words are instruments provides an illuminating framework for understanding all of this, and some guidance in carrying out operations of dissolving problems in a detailed and workmanlike manner.

I will enlarge on this under two headings, both having to do with the aims and methods of philosophy as Wittgenstein would practise it.

3.1 The unmasking of misbegotten questions

We are much inclined to ask questions such as 'What is thinking (or believing or knowing or intending or meaning what we say)?' In asking these questions we are taking it that the words record the existence or the occurrence of something or other in the physical or the mental world, or perhaps spanning both; some action, process, event or state of affairs. Our problem is that, although we use these words all the time, we cannot right away say what kind of a something or other they record. This is surprising. If someone used words such as 'house', 'dog', 'skip' or 'run', and yet not only could not define them but did not know which objects were dogs, or which actions were instances of running, he would be in need of some basic linguistic instruction. But that is not what we are lacking when we ask these philosophical questions. We use words such as 'think', 'believe' and 'intend' competently enough and, if we are in need of anything, it is not instruction in the language, but instruction in thinking about it.

Lacking such instruction, we are apt to suppose that 'I have been thinking' is like 'I have been waltzing.' One could have done a dance, and discover later that it was a waltz, or one could have thought one was waltzing, and realize later that it was some other dance, or no known dance at all. We can correctly or incorrectly identify what we did as waltzing, and we are apt to think that similarly we can be right or wrong about whether what we were just doing was thinking. We suppose that, as with waltzing, there are specifications of thinking, to which what we were just doing might have conformed or failed to conform. We then ask 'But what are they?' and, when we find ourselves unable to say, we still reckon that we must know what they are, since (as we suppose) we so often identify what we did as thinking. We wonder whether perhaps thoughts are ineffable, like the smell of coffee; or whether we may know whether it is *thinking* we are doing in the way we know the rules of a game we have played so often that conforming to its rules has become second nature, and it would now require some effort to formulate what we know. One way or another we do not doubt that we do know what thinking is, but there seems to be work to be done either in composing a statement of what we thus know, or else in explaining why this cannot be done.

Are we not on firm ground so far? There will certainly be room for disagreement when we get to nailing down a claim that thinking is indescribable, or alternatively when we work out a statement of the characteristics by which it is properly identified, but surely we do know what it is, otherwise how could we confidently say so often that we have been doing it? No, 'to think' is not used that way. When we say we have been thinking, we have not identified something that has been happening, by its properties. We *can* make mistakes in using the word 'think', but not the mistake of failing to notice the properties of what we have been doing, or of being careless about how we match what we noticed to a model of thinking. It is incorrect to say 'I have been thinking of taking up hang-gliding' if one is not quite seriously inclined to do this, but if God saw into one's mind when one was fantasizing about rather than thinking about doing this, he need not be able, just from seeing what happened, to tell the difference. People do not say 'What happened can't have been a case of thinking, it was too inexplicit (or too muddled or too anything else that compares what happened with what has to happen for it to be thinking).' There is no such language-game.

There are some fine examples in Hume's *Treatise* of the trouble one can get into through this tendency to suppose that believing, imagining, understanding, remembering are definitely several distinct kinds of something, and then being faced with the question in any given case 'But *what* kind?'. Hume reckoned for example that both understanding a proposition and believing it will be a matter of having something come before the mind, and that the difference, for any given proposition, cannot be a difference in what comes before the mind, otherwise one would be believing something different from what one understood. One can't picture a dog on a raft, or anything other than a cat on a mat, as a way of understanding the proposition that the cat is on the mat. Hence, he concluded, the difference must lie in the *manner* in which the ideas appear, and he said that when we believe, our ideas have a greater force, liveliness, solidity. He said that these words do not adequately convey the difference, but only hint at the peculiar quality of the experience of believing, a quality that can be properly known only in having that experience.

Hume's assumptions did not leave him much room for manoeuvre, and given them his reasoning shows a characteristic shrewdness but, for all that, his conclusions are uncommonly silly. The things we believe are believed whether we are thinking of them or not, and not generally believed more firmly when before the mind. We can picture states of affairs very vividly without in the least believing that they exist, or illustrate to ourselves sketchily a proposition we believe, without supposing that the state of affairs we believe to obtain is sketchy, and we can picture something faintly without having the least doubt that it exists.

Hume had to find some phenomenon that the word 'believe' recorded, and the phenomenon had to have properties that distinguished it from understanding and imagining, without it always being something different that was understood or imagined, and that is how this shrewd sceptic came to hold such a preposterous view. But might his assumptions be sound, and his mistake lie just in the answer he gave to the question? Might belief be some other phenomenon, an act that the mind performs on some of its images perhaps, or maybe a state of the nervous system?

While it might not be surprising if we could not specify exactly what properties a conscious state must have in order to be called a belief, it would be most remarkable if, while we use the word 'believe' routinely, we could not say to which of various entirely different phenomena the word referred: if 'a conscious state', 'a state of the nervous system' and 'a pattern of behaviour' all seemed initially believable answers. It would be as if we were open to the suggestion that a waltz might be a piece of garden furniture, a geometrical theorem or a suba-tomic particle. And yet this is how it is with the word 'believe'.

Why are we so given to supposing that words like 'believe' record something? Perhaps because their surface grammar so resembles that of words that do record something. Some sentences in which the former words occur have the same ring as sentences in which the latter occur. We say 'He said it and I believed it' (a division of labour?). For 'He said it' to be true, something we call saying must have occurred, so we think that similarly, for 'I believed it' to be true, something called believing it must have occurred. We have no great difficulty with what his saying it consisted in, but the parallel question about my believing it seems deeply puzzling.

How is it to be decided whether we are making a mistake in pressing questions like the latter? I suggest that there are two parts to this operation, the second of which involves the conception of words as instruments.

The first part involves comparing the depth grammars of the two words that have been taken to be similar, that is, comparing the broad array of sentences in which each can correctly be used. If, for any sentence in which 'to say' may be used, there is a corresponding sentence in which 'to believe' may be used, then the apparent similarity is confirmed and, if saying is an action, so is believing; while if there are construc-tions with one that do not exist for the other, that argues that they are different kinds of words.

We carry out the operation of comparing depth grammars in ways such as the following: we note that we can say it in English, or menacingly, and can put off saying it, forget to say it, or set about saying it and be interrupted. (Here 'We can. . .'

does not note a human capacity, but a grammatical truth, such as that 'I intended it say it' or 'I forgot to say it' are grammatically in order.) One cannot however believe it in English, or menacingly, and cannot put off believing it, forget to believe it, set about believing it or be interrupted while engaged in believing it. (This does not mean that one can only believe it in some language other than English, or in a friendly manner, or that believing can only be done right away, and so on, but rather that the sentences using the word 'believe' that correspond to sentences using the word 'say' do not have a sense. We do not know what would count as being engaged in believing something.) Hence the fact that 'He said it' is true only if an event called his saying it occurred is not a reason to suppose that 'He believed it' will be true only if an event called his believing it occurred; and the question 'What event is *that*?' does not so far arise.

In this way it can be determined whether 'say' and 'believe' are similar kinds of word; but the answer may be unconvincing, or at least leave us very curious, unless it is followed by an explanation of what kind of word 'believe' *is*. Providing such an explanation is the second part of the operation of determining whether it is a mistake to press a question like what believing is (in the sense of what must occur for 'I believe it' to be true), and the explanation we provide, an explanation of how 'believe' works, not only relieves our curiosity but more importantly enables us to see immediately the mistake the surface grammar has got us into.

When we realize that to say 'I believe what he said' is to do something (namely to mark what he said true, while recognizing room for disagreement), and is not a report of the doing of anything, it is immediately obvious that the condition for its truth, whatever it is, cannot be that something called believing it did occur. We may still be curious about what *are* its truth conditions, but here we are wanting to know more about how it works; and the point that has emerged regarding what they are not is all that is needed to show that the question which phenomenon believing is should not have arisen.

Coming to see how a word works – what kind of instrument it is – plays that kind of role in the larger job of unmasking misbegotten questions.

Here we see the importance of a point I have made, that it is not just whether words are instruments that matters here, but what kind of instrument a particular word is: 'how it works'. Since Wittgenstein seemed to hold that all words are instruments, it would serve no particular purpose to recognize that the word 'believe' is one such. It is when we see *what kind* of instrument it is that a philosophical dividend may accrue.

Performatives and quasi-performatives are two kinds of instrument, and concealed metaphors are a third, and in any of these cases we can see how the detail of what kind of instrument we are looking at can be an unmasking too. For example if minds and consciences are imaginary entities, the conceptions of which we trade on as a way of saying various things about people, it will clearly be a mistake to puzzle over what these entities are, whether there are any of them, how they are related to bodies, or whether perhaps there is nothing but bodies.

If it were discovered that, unbeknown to us, there have all along been immaterial entities, by having one of which we were enabled to calculate and ruminate, it is unlikely that these could be both agile and have backs in which intentions to write letters are located sometimes; and we would not have been demonstrating an intuitive apprehension of their existence when we asked 'What do you have in mind?' or when we described someone as being out of her mind, or being high-minded.

If we were persuaded that minds are imaginary entities, it might seem to follow that there is nothing but bodies; but so to conclude is to remain in the thrall of the mind story. In the story, take away minds and there is nothing but bodies; but to take away minds is just to say that the whole thing is a story, and thus to invalidate the inference, that holds only within the story, that bodies are all that remain. The question whether there are only bodies would hardly arise but for the mind story but, when it is posed, if it cannot be turned off with the questions 'Why ever would you suppose that?' or 'What are you meaning to exclude?', it might best be handled by discussing how the supposition squares with the existence of empty spaces, shadows, rainbows, mirror images, hurricanes, proofs, poems, addictions and pains.

3.2 Relieving the urge to reform language

The shape of language can certainly change, and some changes may be reckoned improvements, other not. Our new-found sensitivity to male chauvinism has led us to perceive the need for a personal pronoun that would fit in the same slots as 'he' and 'she' but be sexless, and for a sexless adjective that could be used in the place of 'his' and 'her'.

It would be a happy turn of events if words to fill these bills emerged and came to be used as routinely as most other words. As things stand this part of our language sometimes gives us a choice between sounding sexist and writing inelegantly; but no case arises here for saying that language is *inaccurate*. There is a need for sexless pronouns and adjectives, not because there are people who are neither male nor female (perhaps there are, but it is not in order to talk about *them* that we want the new words), but because we sometimes have occasion to speak about people collectively, without reference to their sex. Instead of saying 'A student must have his or her application in by 15 May' (God help us!), a word like 'shiz' might come to replace the heavy-handed 'his or her', just as, in some circles, 'Ms' has come to be used in place of 'Miss' or Mrs' when we disapprove of the practice of routinely marking the marital status of women, but not of men.

I have been describing ways in which language changes. A need is perceived, some people start using a coined word or expression in a way that fills the need, and the practice catches on. In other cases there is no widely recognized need, but someone perhaps more or less whimsically extends the application of a word, and the development is found charming or useful, and may settle into the language. There might have been a time when 'hard to believe' struck people as being a quaint conception, suggesting that believing is a task, the performance of which might require skill or diligence; but still the expression might have appealed to people as a way of saying that a proposition is implausible, and might have taken root so thoroughly that now one's attention needs to be drawn to its strangeness, and we are no longer inclined to smile when we use it.

What is at stake in developments of this kind is not truth or accuracy, but convenience, style, charm or moral principle. 'He or she' and 'his or her' do the job perfectly well, they just grate on the ear. The changes are not required for a truer understanding of what we are talking about, but reflect our tastes, interests, attitudes. If there is discussion of them it will be over coffee or in letters to the editors of newspapers, not in philosophical journals or seminars in linguistics. (*I* am discussing them, but not participating in arguments for or against any particular changes, just noting the nature of the phenomenon.)

Philosophers sometimes think in a quite different way about language and the desirability of changing it. They grumble at language for enshrining misunderstandings of the way things are or, if they do not go so far as to register specific objections of this kind, they at least think there is a question for investigation whether the words of our language accurately reflect the way things are. They think it is the duty of language to do this. Here they are urging, not that we restrict our assertions to those that are true, but rather that we purify language until none of its words gives rise to misunderstandings about how things are.

If we say the sun rose this morning at 6.05, that may well be true, but our words suggest something we do not believe, namely that the earth stands still and the sun is in motion and, if the sun is as far away as we believe it to be, it travels at enormous speeds. We now learn at an early age not to be deceived by this particular expression and some others; but one might well become anxious about whether there are large numbers of other expressions that are equally misleading, but the erroneousness of the connotations of which has not been noticed. It seems antecedently unlikely that a language that largely came into being before Newton, Freud or Einstein will be a proper mirror of the way things are. Language has no doubt changed since Newton's time, but mostly not in ways that have any connection with his theories, and the same for Freud and Einstein. We still say that the sun rises, that our consciences bother us, that events occur simultaneously.

Even if we do not know how to decide whether language has kept pace with scientific developments, it can be a nagging worry, not only that this may well be true, but (if language itself, as distinct from the assertions we make using it, is capable of falsely mirroring reality) that would almost certainly be true.

Carrying the anxiety a step further, one can even feel oneself to be at all times the pawn of language. Whatever I think about, including whether there may be a linguistic lag, my thinking may be hobbled by the crude medium in which it is conducted. This is an anxiety for which there seems no remedy: if one were to try to construct a shining new language, one would be defining its terms in English or German or some other imperfect tongue, and it would be infected with the imperfections of that tongue. (Thus Berkeley, who was doomed like the rest of us to write in English or some other language, regarded himself as at least able to *think* without words, and desperately recommended that we make his words the occasion of wordless thoughts of our own. And he was not averse to saying such things as that although, owing to the crude ordinary use of the word 'idea', it 'sounds very harsh' to say that we eat, drink and are clothed with ideas, still that is certainly true, since we are fed and clothed with those things we perceive immediately by our senses, and we in fact never perceive anything but ideas [*Principles*, Introduction §§22, 25; §38].)

Wittgenstein was clearly interested in concerns of this kind, and may at first appear to have a contradictory stance on these matters. On the one hand he says such things as that 'Philosophy is a battle against the bewitchment of our intelligence by means of language' (*PI* §109), while on the other he says '. . . it is clear that every sentence in our language "is in order as it is"' (*PI* §98). And one wants to know how language can be deemed to be 'in order', if it bewitches our intelligence? (One can also be bewitched by what cunning or unscrupulous people say, but Wittgenstein seems to be countering the fear that we shall be bewitched by *whatever* anyone says, because it will be said in *words*, and they are bewitching.)

The point that every sentence in our language is in order as it is is less striking than it may at first appear, when one remembers that to be a sentence in the language *is* to be in order. 'It is five o'clock on the sun' or 'I have understood it continuously since yesterday' are not 'sentences in the language' as Wittgenstein seems to use that expression, since they are not in order. But in *PI* §120 there seems to be an argument that a new language could not express anything that could not be made clear by careful use of the language of everyday, and hence, if ordinary language is not all right, at least there is no cure for this.

Is [the language of every day] somehow too coarse and

material for what we want to say? *Then how is another to be constructed?* – And how strange that we should be able to do anything at all with the one we have! (*PI* §120)

The conflict that seems to arise here is not difficult to resolve, however. Just as it can be true that the sun rose this morning at 6.05, although these words falsely suggest that the earth stands still and the sun moves, it can be true that I meant what I said, or that I believed what she said, although these forms of expression falsely suggest that something happened that *was* my meaning it or believing it.

Instead of reforming language, Wittgenstein wants to teach us how to expose and destroy linguistic illusions. When we do this, the language that gave rise to the illusions will remain, and be 'in order'. It may be that, no matter how much we refine these skills, we shall always be in danger of being deceived by the language we use, but we shall at least have at our disposal means of protecting ourselves.

The analogy with statements about sunrisings may be misleading. In all probability the expression 'the sun rose' came into use when and because people believed that the earth stood still and the sun moved, and although cosmological investigations later showed that belief to be false, the old way of speaking lingered on; but there could hardly have been a time when people falsely believed that something significant sometimes occurred when they said or heard or read something, and they fell into the way of calling these occurrences 'believing it'. Before the word 'believe' came into use, there was nothing to generate that illusion. There are non-linguistic facts (such as that we do not see or feel the earth moving) that generate the illusion that it stands still and the sun moves; and the illusion antedated the expression 'the sun rises'. But there is nothing but language that generates the illusion that meaning something or believing something are events, and the illusion could not antedate the emergence of these words.

Since these illusions are not generated by any psychological or physical phenomena, they do not stand to be corrected by psychological or physical investigations. And since they *are* generated by language, they stand to be corrected by linguistic investigations.

However the corrections need not consist in devising new ways of speaking. It will be enough if we as it were write footnotes to the existing expressions that confuse us. We do not after all get the wrong message if someone says she meant it or she believed it. It is not as if she had said something ambiguous. It is only when we stop and reflect on some of the expressions we use (when language goes on holiday,) that we suppose she was reporting something that happened, and find it puzzling what event that could be. And it is only then that the 'footnotes' are needed.

Parts of this sketch of how Wittgenstein viewed these matters may be seen in the following passages:

> Our investigation is . . . a grammatical one. Such an investigation sheds light on our problem by clearing misunderstandings away. Misunderstandings concerning the use of words, caused, among other things, by certain analogies between the forms of expression in different regions of language. (*PI* §90)

> Philosophy may in no way interfere with the actual use of language; it may in the end only describe it.

> For it cannot give it any foundation either.

> It leaves everything as it is. (*PI* §124)

> It was true to say that our considerations could not be scientific ones. It was not of any possible interest to us to find out empirically 'that, contrary to our preconceived ideas, it is possible to think such-and-such' – whatever that may mean. (*PI* §109)

> We want to establish an order in our knowledge of the use of language . . . . This may make it look as if we saw it as our task to reform language.

> Such a reform for particular practical purposes, an improvement in our terminology designed to prevent misunderstandings in practice, is perfectly possible. But these are not the cases we have to do with. The confusions which occupy us arise when language is like an engine idling, not when it is doing work. (*PI* §132)

These passages *declare* a view, rather than arguing for it and, while I know of no place where Wittgenstein specifically defends the position so declared, clearly he would have a defence of it in aspects of my interpretation of the idea that words are instruments. If concepts reflect our nature and are neither accurate nor inaccurate representations of the way things are, if it is the assertions we make that have a duty to be accurate (*PI* §241), not the concepts we have, it will be absurd to worry that possibly our concepts are inaccurate, or to look to improving their accuracy by investigating the objects (if any) they are concepts of.

Epilogue

DEFENCE OF THESE PHILOSOPHICAL METHODS

Much of the perennial impatience with Wittgenstein arises from people having no clear grasp of what his aims are or how he goes about pursuing them. If this is true, at least part of the remedy must lie in presenting a clear and attractive picture of what it is to transact philosophical business in a Wittgensteinian fashion. That is what I have been trying to do.

Someone who found my 'picture' clear enough, and interesting, might still have doubts about whether I have given enough reason to identify it with Wittgenstein. I think it is uncommonly difficult to be quite sure one has understood Wittgenstein, but I think it would have to be admitted that my exegetical arguments at least provide a good deal of support for a claim to have understood. If anyone at least found that my 'picture' constituted an attractive and workable philosophical programme, I would not be dissatisfied with that outcome. I do not use the claim that my picture accurately represents Wittgenstein as evidence that it is a sound way of transacting philosophical business; and if such a person was in any case inclined to do philosophy in the ways described, and had acquired some proficiency at this, I would let her be as anti-Wittgenstein as she liked, especially if she made it very clear what she opposed as being Wittgensteinian, and exactly how it differed from her own way of handling philosophical difficulties.

A more specific objection that is often voiced is that whether or not I have described a workable programme – as it were, a game, in which there really are winning and losing strategies – still the business that is carried on in philosophy as I describe it can have nothing to do with how things are, because it is all based on the study of natural language, which has taken shape over hundreds of years and at the hands of

people many of whom were ignorant, undiscerning or super-
stitious. There is no reason, it might be argued, to suppose that
such a legacy enshrines any insights into what there is, or
anything else that philosophers have wanted to know. If in
studying language someone hit on something that seemed
important, it would not be because that point was enshrined
in language that it would be regarded as an insight, but
because independently of language it was discovered to be
sound. So, the argument might run, the most the study of
language could contribute would be a set of leads, some of
which might prove to be fruitful. We may indeed study it with
such a rather desperate hope in view, the way contemporary
medical researchers sometimes experiment with herbal reme-
dies, to see if perhaps our ancestors hit on something important, but it will be contemporary investigations that establish
the value of an old remedy, and similarly it will be investigations independent of language that show in any particular
case whether what language led us to suspect is true.

It should by now be fairly obvious that, if my reading of
Wittgenstein is at all along the right lines, this objection shows
a total misunderstanding of his conception of philosophy. He
did not earnestly pose questions such as 'What is thinking?',
'What are minds?', and so on, and then for unimaginable
reasons proceed to answer them by studying the way the
words 'think', 'mind' and so on are used. He did recommend
studying the use of such words, but not with a view to
discovering anything about the nature of the objects to which
they may seem to refer: rather, to find out whether there are
such objects, and if so which objects they are (*PI* §373).

(We do not study language to find out whether there are
dogs, or hyacinths; but then we *know* there are dogs and
hyacinths. When we were young, people told us 'That's a dog',
and 'That is, too'; and made routine references to 'that dog
over there', and so on. In that way our concept of a dog was
shaped. There will never be learned articles on whether it
might be a myth that there are dogs. But we cannot similarly
say there is just no doubt that there are minds; no one has told
us 'That's a mind, and so is that'; and while we do make
routine references to minds, for example in describing this
person's mind as lazy, and that person's as restless, it will not
be our having noticed one person's mind failing to get to work
on a problem he has, or the other's skipping aimlessly from

one topic to another, that leads us to say such things; and a person used to the way we talk about dogs and hyacinths may well be perplexed by the absence when it comes to minds of the thing that is lazy or restless.)

Wittgenstein was not trying to *answer* traditional philosophical questions, but to show that we make a mistake in asking them. He was not in the business of basing conclusions about how things are on the study of language, and the objections that this cannot be done would not alarm him in the least, even if it pained him to be thought so stupid as to believe otherwise.

If, as I have suggested, his response to the question what minds are would be that there is no reason to suppose that they are anything, because the word 'mind', unlike the word 'liver', is not used to refer to anything – there is nothing called a mind that we might investigate – Wittgenstein would simply have no need for the supposition that there is wisdom enshrined in the language of everyday.

Neither does he study the use of words in the hope of finding out what minds, thoughts, hopes, and so on are at least *believed* to be. There is no implicit argument that 200,000,000 anglophones could not be wrong about what a thought is, for example. He is not basing philosophical conclusions on vulgar prejudices, or sophisticated prejudices either. A landlubber might, by watching and listening to sailors, come to the conclusion that the tiller is that bit of wood they steer the thing with. But the landlubber is a stranger to sailors' language, while Wittgenstein in no way plays the role of a stranger to any language he speaks, and does nothing analogous to reckoning that, since Peter moved that bit of wood to the right when asked to move the tiller to the right, the bit of wood must be the tiller.

People who earnestly say that surely we should find out what anything is, not by studying the word that is used to refer to it, but by studying the thing itself, not only have not yet taken the point that we are not in the business of finding out what anything is, but have not yet faced up to the problem that, in the cases that puzzle us, we do not yet know which phenomena, if any, to investigate as being a mind, a belief, an intention. . . .

A question such as 'What is a mind?' might be in order if treated as a crude way of asking what minds are made of, how they work, what effects they have on thoughts or bodies or what have you. These are questions that we might investigate, provided only that there was some identifiable (if perhaps obscure) object that we all called the mind. It would be like the crudely put question 'What is a pineal gland?', asked when we already knew which organ was that gland, and we just wanted to know what purpose it served, how it worked, and so on. Similarly, if it had long been known that there was something that hovered just over people's heads, and glowed in the dark or emitted gamma rays, and if it had always been called the mind, we might wonder whether it was a magnetic field, a cloud of some gas, or what; whether it served some purpose in the human constitution and if so what purpose, and by virtue of what design feature it performed its function. We could sum up our curiosity about these matters in the question 'what is a mind?', but to make headway with our investigation we would have in another sense already to know what minds are: they are that well-known glowing area that we see in the dark above people's heads.

It would be wrong in that case to say that people *believed* that the glowing areas were minds, as if we all might be mistaken about this. Everyone who understood the language would say the same; a person who did not know would be in need of linguistic instruction, as would someone who did not know what a gyroscope was; and if anyone said minds are not that glowing area over people's heads, but are brains or thoughts or anything else, she would just be wrong, and could be shown to be so by consulting a dictionary.

It might be that in Australia or California they had a different name for these glowing areas, just as what North Americans call elevators, Britons call lifts, but these divergences would be sorted out in simple ways and there would be no question for investigation, whether the glowing areas really are minds.

That question *could* arise if (a) the glowing areas were not standardly called minds, and (b) the word 'mind' had a different use, meaning for example 'whatever it may turn out to be that enables us to calculate'. In that case whether the glowing areas are minds would be a serious question, on which we could get to work. It would mean 'Is it through having these glowing areas that we are able to calculate.

If someone like Hume or G. E. Moore tells us that minds are

desires and fears and thoughts and memories, either he will be making a semantic point, the correctness of which can be investigated, or he will simply be proposing to call the study of desires and so on the study of minds. In that case he will not be able to claim to be *right* about what minds are, and could not be accused of being wrong either.

What will show what, if anything, boojums are is an investigation of whether the word 'boojum' is used to allude to any known entity. This is a question how the word 'boojum' works, what kind of instrument it is. Such questions are prior to any empirical inquiries. In most cases they are unnecessary. If I want to know whether counteracting acid rain with antacids would produce an excess of harmful substances in rivers and lakes, there will not likely be an underlying conceptual problem, but if I wonder whether intentions cause actions, there will right away be a question whether intentions are the sort of thing that *could* cause actions, or anything else.

We might, as some philosophers seem to do, take it that we do not need to know what intentions are, because whenever anyone truthfully says she is intending to do something, *whatever intentions may be* there will certainly be an intention there. That assumes however that we use the word 'intend' to record the presence of something; and if that assumption were mistaken it would not be clear that there was anything called an intention that people who have intentions have, that might serve as a cause of actions.

The question whether intentions are something cannot be investigated by examining ourselves when we intend. If we do that, we shall likely find all sorts of things, but whether any of them or any assortment of them is an intention will depend on whether it is routinely so called – and in fact there is nothing we call the intention we had to stop for a beer on the way home.

It is true that most of the time people are in no way embarrassed to say they are intending such and such, but that does not show they believe there is such a phenomenon as intending. They just use words, and do not have or need theories about how they work.

It is *philosophers*, who, reflecting on what people say, conclude that folks believe that intending (or what have you) *occurs*, and proceed from there to conclude democratically that therefore it does occur, or undemocratically that it does not, and perhaps that we have been deluded into thinking that anyone ever intends anything. As if they knew without investigation what intending would be if there was any of it, and found that in fact it never occurred.

Another frequently voiced objection to linguistic analysis is that, either many linguistic truths are not transcultural, or at least that much-needed demonstrations of transculturality are not even attempted in the works of linguist analysts. The objection is that this makes philosophy a very localized affair. Problems that arise for anglophones may not arise for people who speak Chinese or Kwakiutl.

If we are in the business, not of discovering how things are, but of exposing illusions generated by language, the work we do will be helpful to more people, the more languages there are that generate a particular illusion; but there may still be useful work to be done if only one or only five of the world's languages generate a certain grammatical illusion, especially if there are lots of other such illusions, waiting to be exposed.

The objection here is sometimes raised, not in the above form, but as a further argument against basing conclusions about the nature of things on language. If languages differ in any fundamental ways, then the conclusions about what there is that are based on them will vary from one language to the next, and we might have on our hands as many realities as there are languages. Clearly this argument rests on the mis-taken supposition that Wittgensteinian philosophers are trying to make discoveries about the nature of things through study-ing language.

It might however be argued that we in fact do reach conclu-sions about the nature of things, for example when we argue that there is nothing that was Peter's meaning Martha when he spoke of a friend who has a nice old wooden ketch. It may be that the conclusions linguistic philosophers reach here are all negative, but still we are saying something about reality when we say it does not include meaning Martha, or meaning by a ketch a sailing craft with the mizzen mast forward of the rudder post.

The point would be a good one if it were clear what the phenomenon of meaning Martha would be if there were such phenomena. Then we would know what we were subtracting from reality, or denying to reality in saying that there was nothing that Peter's meaning Martha consisted in. It would be like saying there are no lakes and no tobacco plants on the moon. In that case we know what is alleged to be lacking; but if we have no conception what the phenomenon of meaning Martha would be, saying there is nothing that is meaning her subtracts precisely nothing from reality. It is like denying that there are boojums on the Queen Charlotte Islands.

Normally if I say I meant so-and-so, that will be *true*, but that is not to say that as well as saying I meant so-and-so, something called meaning so-and-so will have occurred. If there were such a phenomenon, it might occur for example when I was talking about wooden ketches. I could report that I was saying how much work wooden boats are to maintain when suddenly I meant Charlie. It would either be providential or the result of long training that such things never happened.

A quite different objection that is often voiced is that the ways words are used are too variable and flexible to provide a solid foundation for any philosophical conclusion. 'Soon' can, in the context of when supper will be ready, mean 'in the next ten minutes', but in the context of when the world's supply of fossil fuels will be almost exhausted, it can mean 'within forty years'. 'Nice' is often opposed to 'naughty' but, if what someone has said is not just of the sort we would call a nice point, it is not therefore naughty. Somewhat differently, some philosopher somewhere is sure to have said that the question whether we did something voluntarily can arise only when the action in question would generally be deemed discreditable; while others would quite unabashedly say that someone quite voluntarily contributed a large sum of money to such and such a (good) cause.

Some of these points do not at all show what they are alleged to show. There is no significant disagreement about whether 'soon' might mean 'in about ten minutes' in one context, but 'in about forty years' in another; and the person who says that only of discreditable acts can the question arise whether they were voluntary is shown by the counterexample not just to have a conflicting opinion but to be *wrong*.

But there is a more general answer to this tired old objection: that although we are all liable at one time or another, in our anxiety to support some contention, to make a point that turns out to be flabby, ample points are often available that do not fall to this kind of criticism. No one says 'I was intending to go to Montreal when suddenly the phone rang'; no one says

'I made a dire threat, but I was so worked up I quite forgot to mean it'; no one asks multi-lingual people in what language they believed it would rain soon; no one wonders whether what she was doing just now was thinking; and no one says he has understood the ontological argument unremittingly since yesterday.

The reason we do not say these things is not that the states of affairs they may appear to describe either do not occur or are of so little interest that we do not bother to mention them: but that we make no sense of the sentences in question. We have no idea what could have been happening just before the phone rang, that we would call 'intending to go to Montreal'; we do not know how we would set about meaning a threat that it suddenly occurred to us we had neglected to mean; believing is not a verbal action, the way threatening may be, and only of verbal actions would it make sense to ask in what language they were performed; and so on.

It is sometimes objected that sense *can* be made of many of these sentences that are alleged to be meaningless. If someone says she forgot to intend to go to the bank today, we can see what she probably means: she forgot to list it on her agenda. If someone says that, after saying Peter is coming, for a whole minute he meant Peter McNiven, what happened was probably that for a minute he thought about that Peter, and so on. Clearly though these sentences do not mean what we may guess their authors mean by them. They have simply made understandable mistakes in their handling of some English words.

It may be only in common rooms or seminars that points such as that one cannot forget to intend are made, but those points do not therefore reflect just the sophisticated linguistic tastes of those who take note of them. Cab drivers, poets and politicians alike will understand if you say you are intending to go to Montreal, but not if you say intending to go there was going on just as you crossed Queen street. No one will have difficulty understanding you if you make a threat and say you mean it, but no matter to whom you are speaking, if you say you forgot to mean it, perplexity will arise, and so on. Some busy people will not bend their minds to such questions, and when interviewed will not understand the question, and may just say whatever they think you want to hear; but if we get people interested, and make what we are asking sufficiently clear, they will soon see that generally there are no two ways of answering. We do not have to settle for the off-hand say-so of non-intellectuals, whatever it may be. If a cabbie were to say that when he is intending to do something he pictures himself doing it, he could be reminded that he does not do this picturing continuously over the time when he has such an intention as to quit early and see a football game, but that he would not care to say that at the time when he was not picturing himself at the game, he was not intending to go.

A somewhat crafty way of setting Wittgenstein aside, and just getting ahead with philosophy as one prefers to do it, is to say that he was wonderful and was badly needed, but that now the work of clearing away the rubble and the cobwebs has been substantially done, and it is not too soon to get on with other things. This way one might save oneself the trouble of raising and defending objections to the whole threatening business; but to talk thankfully about the work of purification having been done fails to recognize that what we stand to acquire from Wittgenstein is not a catalogue of grammatical illusions and proofs that they are such, that we might keep handy and consult whenever we feared we were under the spell of some word, but rather a skill at protecting ourselves from, and at helping others to see, the subtle ways in which language may bewitch us. We shall need this sensitivity if, as proposed, we push on to other business; but if we say we regard the characteristically Wittgensteinian contribution to philosophy as having been made, we are at least very likely to venture into new terrain, not cautiously and with all sensors tuned and turned on, but boldly, confident that the good doctor Wittgenstein has made the territory quite safe. So, trusting that all the atrocious tomfoolery about meanings has been exposed and put to rest, we may start a new era of 'getting on with it' by addressing ourselves to questions such as 'What, after all, are meanings, if, as Wittgenstein has shown us, they are not this and not that. . . ?'

Questions about the nature of philosophy are peculiarly difficult to argue over, but most philosophers will at least not be happy with the idea that philosophy is from first to last the business, not of answering questions or solving problems, but of showing the questions and problems we have to be based on misunderstandings. It is not perfectly clear whether Wittgenstein is committed to such a view. He does at least seem to be saying in part that whenever a certain kind of question leaves us at a loss, it will turn out to be misbegotten. I will need to say something about what this 'certain kind' of question is; but right away we can see that given this much there will be two large areas in which there may remain genuine questions: (i) if it is only *a certain kind* of question that is going to turn out to be misbegotten, there may clearly remain questions that are not of that kind. Whether these are still philosophical questions many need investigation, but at least the answer is not settled by anything laid down so far. (ii) The question 'Does this question rest on a mistake?' will not itself be a misbegotten question, and further will not be answered just by showing that the question referred to is of this 'certain kind'.

What is this 'certain kind' of question? It is one that we would expect to be readily answerable, but that surprisingly leaves us at a loss. Augustine was surprised to find that, although when no one asked him, he knew what time was, when the question what it is was posed, he was unable to say. Similarly it may seem remarkable that although it is clear that some people have a conscience and others do not, we seem not to know what a conscience is. We expect a question like Augustine's to be readily answerable because we understand questions like what time is it, or how long it will be until sun-up, and yet (we think) we surely could not understand these if we did not know what time is. There might not be this worry if the problem were only that we found it hard to define the word 'time', but whereas without being able to define the word 'dog' we may correctly identify animals as dogs, and in that sense know what a dog is, there is not even anything we correctly identify as time.

There are some questions, such as 'What is the chemical composition of the powder in this jar?', that we *expect* to be difficult to answer. It is in no way disturbing if we do not know the answer right away, or even if we do not know how to work out the answer. Unless we are chemists, there is no reason to expect that we should have these abilities; but when we use words like 'time', 'mind' or 'intend' every day and apparently quite competently, it is remarkable, not only that we should be unable to explain what they mean, but that we should be unable to present ourselves with uncontroversial examples.

Concerning this kind of question, did Wittgenstein hold

that we shall always turn out to be making a mistake in asking it? He did not declare himself on this, but it does sound as if he did so hold, for example when he says such sweeping things as that 'philosophy is the battle against the bewitchment of our intelligence by means of language' (*PI* §109). However we would be battling such bewitchment to the hilt if we always considered searchingly whether our difficulty might arise through misunderstanding what kind of a word we were dealing with (and had some skill at answering such a question) – even if we found that only in one case in ten did our puzzlement prove to rest on a mistake. There are no cases I know of in which Wittgenstein examines an apparently fishy question and finds it to be in order but, just as an intern in a hospital emergency ward may go a long time without finding a patient not in need of treatment, the impression of universality that Wittgenstein generates in this way may have arisen only from his being in the business of unmasking questions it is a mistake to ask.

Wittgenstein was clearly not logically bound to say there are no healthy philosophical questions. He might of course say that, if a question is healthy, it is therefore not philosophical; but not only would this discredit his own questions, it would make the work done in answering them otiose, since the answer in any particular case would be a foregone conclusion.

Whatever Wittgenstein may have believed about this issue, I suggest the healthiest arrangement would be one in which all philosophers, regardless what sort of problems they proposed to concentrate on, were given enough training in detecting bogus questions to enable them to manage for themselves most of the time, but in which there were also watchdogs, people who had shown themselves particularly zealous and adept in these matters, to whom anyone could apply for advice in hard cases. The dogs, being only canine, might sometimes make exaggerated claims, and might be found obnoxious in other ways, sticking their noses into other's business, sometimes robbing colleagues of problems very dear to them, and betimes declaring that except in the watchdogs' part of philosophy there is nothing but muddle-headedness; but the wise generality of philosophers would bear with all this unpleasantness, because after all who would want to struggle and strain for long years over problems that would

never have arisen if we were all as good at avoiding bewitchment by language as not very many of us are?

INDEXES

Index of Topics

Index of Passages Cited or Discussed

Indexes